FROM GEEK TO PEAK:

YOUR FIRST 365 DAYS

AS A TECHNICAL

CONSULTANT

BY THOMAS MYER

NIMBLE BOOKS LLC

Nimble Books LLC

ISBN-13: 978-1-934840-56-6

ISBN-10: 1-934840-56-4

Copyright 2008 Thomas Myer

Version 1.0; last saved 2009-02-06.

Nimble Books LLC

1521 Martha Avenue

Ann Arbor, MI 48103-5333

http://www.nimblebooks.com

The cover font, heading fonts and the body text inside the book are in Constantia, designed by John Hudson for Microsoft.

Contents

ACKNOWLEDGEMENTS

Dedicated to my wife Hope, who loves me anyway.

NIMBLE BOOKS LLC

CHAPTER 1: INTRODUCTION

Let's make a deal, right here, right now.

I'll start with a promise. This is not going to be your usual book about starting a business. It won't contain any familiar chestnuts about choosing a snazzy business name, buying a Yellow Pages ad, hiring a graphic designer to create a pimpin' logo, and doing everything you can to be the hottest thing on the scene. It's going to deliver realistic, targeted advice for the technical professional seeking to make his or her own way as a freelancer or consultant. In fact, it's going to focus on your first 365 days in business, because that's where you lay all the groundwork for your career.

What's more, 90% of the advice will be centered on marketing yourself as a technical professional, using techniques that will build your visibility and credibility. Because I know most of you hate marketing, I make a further solemn promise to give you the kind of advice that won't make you feel like a jackass when you follow it.

That's my part of the deal.

What's your part?

It's simple, really. Before you proceed, you're going to agree to a simple little thing. It's not such a big thing at first glance, but by agreeing to it, you make yourself ready to absorb what's in this book. We only have a few hours together, but in those few hours, I hope to make your first year in business a roaring success.

Okay, here's what you have to agree to:

My name is [insert name here] and I am a complete and total ninja bad-ass in [insert name of technical prowess here].

Read that line a few more times to yourself, then say it out loud a few times. Walk up to your nearest significant other (if you have more than one, then all righty), spouse (ditto), brother, sister, parent, dog, or just a mirror and say it. Then repeat it a few more times, but mean it this time. Don't read another friggin' word of this book until you've got that down.

If you're in a bookstore just leafing through this thing, trying to decide if you want to buy it or maybe splurge your hard-earned bucks on a John Mellencamp retrospective instead, go ahead and do it anyway. Just walk up to a store clerk or that really cute guy/girl in the next aisle. Go ahead. I'll be here when you get back.

If you're incapable of saying it to yourself or others, then I have some bad news for you. You'd better get to the point where you can say it, and believe it, and live it, and BE it, or your career in technical consulting will be awfully nasty, brutish, and short, to paraphrase Hobbes.

Don't despair, though, if you're too scared to say it to someone else. Not yet. Just say it under your breath a couple dozen times. By the end of this book, you will be saying it to everyone. You'll be chomping at the bit to say it. I promise.

If you can say it out loud, right here, right now on this very first page of this book, congratulations! You've taken the first step. As the Consultant to the Consultants (Alan Weiss) once said to a group of us who had gathered to hear him speak in Austin, Texas, the biggest obstacle to consulting success is ... low self-esteem.

You have got to BELIEVE that you are a bad ass in whatever it is you do, because if you do, then others will believe it too, and what's more they will hire you to be the bad ass you are, and tell a whole bunch of other folks, "Man, I just met a complete bad-ass ninja ronin." And pretty soon, people will just come up to you and say, "I hear you're a total ninja bad-ass" and you'll say, "That's right—how can I help you?"

For all of you who are skeptical, let me assure you that I'm not some kind of twit who believes in pat, over generalized solutions, but I have to tell you that this approach does work, and that everything else is just details ... which is where this book comes in. I will show you how to go from cubicle-dwelling geek to self-employed badass, the kind of guy or girl that gets asked out to lunch by harried colleagues who want to know Just How You Do It.

Any questions so far? Well then, let me introduce myself.

A SHORT BIO

I'd hate it if some stranger just walked up to me and started telling me what I'm doing wrong. I would want to know who the stranger is before I started following orders. Hence, my need to introduce myself to you in this section. I'll keep it short and entertaining (like my little Yorkie, Marlowe), but by the end of it I hope you'll know a little more about the messenger, and why the message is so important.

My name is Thomas Myer. I was well on my way to a PhD when, in the spring of 1995 I went to the graduate library and discovered that the school had just purchased and set up two brand new Silicon Graphics workstations. They both had Mosaic loaded on them, and the one closest to me had some kind of document loaded on it: gray background, words on it, some of them underlined in blue and red.

I stopped dead in my tracks, my research forgotten. I stared at the screen for a bit, knowing intuitively that this was something different, something interesting. Much more interesting than whatever it was I was doing at the moment. So I sat down and took control of the mouse.

I knew instinctively that the links were clickable, that they would lead me to other documents. So I gave it a try, and presto, I was somewhere else. It wasn't a particularly interesting destination—just a list of links to anthropology journals, but I kept clicking, and eventually, I crossed the border from academia into a corporate web site. Over the next three or four hours, I traversed several hundred web sites, including several that showed you how to work with HTML.

To make a long story short, the Web had me at hello. I finished my master's degree, and as soon as I could, started working as a book editor in San Antonio. That job gave me a chance to meet some folks working at a little security startup, and I joined them as a junior technical writer. My first job in high-tech was basically sitting at the feet of incredibly smart UNIX ninjas and drinking from the fire hose of information they pointed at me with equal measures of merciless superiority and geeky humor.

At about the same time, my boss in the marketing department asked if I knew anything about web sites, and I said HELL YES and so I also became interim web master.

Fast forward a few years and find me working for a Fortune 50 giant that absorbed the little startup from San Antonio. Now I'm a senior technical writer and working on some XML/SGML initiatives. Along the way I've picked up some mad Perl and UNIX shell scripting skills. I meet even more scary smart people.

A few years later, I'm working for one of the poster children of the dot-bomb era, working as a technical writer and information architect. Turns out I was one of the few guys around who could talk geek to the geeks, marketing to the business stakeholders, and content to the content developers, so I was this glorified air traffic controller helping them get a partner portal off the ground.

Well, all good things come to an end, and mine came when the dot-coms hit the wall. I volunteered myself to be part of the seventh round of layoffs in six months. This was May 2001, and I was about to turn 30. I hadn't had a real vacation in years. I was fed up with all the administrivia, the complete bullshit-artist approach to doing business ("just put Java and XML in the proposal, we'll land the deal!" and my favorite "we lose a penny a transaction, but we'll make up for it in volume!"), the hype and let downs, all the good people let go just so a select few could rake in the stock options.

My plan was very simple: sit on my tired ass and collect my severance package for six weeks, then live off the 100 days of accrued vacation, then tap my 401(k) if I had to, just as long as I had a chance to think. I'd been running on fumes for years, and it was time to recharge.

Two days into my little "wake-up-late, shower-when-I-feel-like-it, wear-jammies-all-day" experiment, I got a call from a local interactive agency. "Hey, we have this client in Colorado that needs help with some information architecture, how would you like to help out?"

I said sure, but in my heart of hearts I didn't want to do it. When they asked how much I charged, I gave them what I thought would be a suitably high, suitably scary number: $75 an hour. They didn't even blink. I got a contract and plane tickets couriered to my house that afternoon, and for a month I shuttled back and forth to Colorado.

On one of those flights back and forth between the stultifying summer heat of Austin and the clear, cool air in Longmont, CO, it dawned on me that consulting is what I should be doing. Think about it! It offered everything I wanted out of my work life. I could get good pay, variety in projects and clients, the chance to make a real difference with clients instead of just being a cog in some corporate contraption hell-bent on using me up like the little cubicle slave I was.

When I got back from the gig, I turned 30 (my wife threw me a surprise birthday party) and I did just that. Looking back, I could just slap myself for being such a naïve wretch. I had no idea what I was getting into, didn't understand business, certainly didn't really fully comprehend the full measure of the journey I was about to embark on.

From the very beginning, I made every single stinkin' mistake in the book, and then proceeded to add some new ones. You'll learn the sordid details in these pages. Rest assured that when I say it's generally a waste of time to get a snazzy logo before you have a paying customer, believe me when I tell you that I learned it through bruising experience.

At the time of this writing, I've been self-employed for seven years and change. In that time, I've been part of a partnership, a sole proprietorship, and an S-corporation. I've worked in a spare bedroom, a broom closet in a downtown Victorian building marketed as an office, another little office in a side wing of an art gallery, as a semi-legal subtenant in a swanky downtown loft office right above a stinky Irish bar, in an office space wholly rented by my company, then back into my spare bedroom. I've gone from having zero employees, to a part-time helper and contractors, to a staff of five, back to just working by myself with contractors to help me. I started out as a PC/Blackberry man and am now a fervent Mac guy, with pimped out MacBook Pro and iPhone.

I've built web sites and written copy for stay-at-home micropreneurs, written PHP applications for Fortune 100 giants, and worked for just about every type of business in between. I once wrote five technical white papers for a giant technology company (one of those with a three-letter acronym for a name) in the space of eight days.

I've worked for dream clients who have a great sense of humor, a good angle on what they want to accomplish, and fantastic communication skills. I've worked for complete and total jackasses who verbally abuse the hired help and who never wrote a check that didn't bounce. And plenty of folks, good and bad in their own ways, in between. I've gotten good at identifying the losers and staying away from them; if stalked, I make sure that they only get me for a pretty price, but even that took me a few times to get right.

Looking back, I can only imagine that I've managed, through insanely long work hours and my fair share of luck, to stay ahead. But it's been enough to survive long enough to write this story, instead of becoming another sad little footnote in the history of freelancers going broke before they break free.

I'm going to do my best to arm you for your first year in business. My hope is that you learn from my experience, and that you won't make any mistakes at all. Of course, that's impossible. At best, you'll avoid all my mistakes but make a few of your own. That's okay—making mistakes isn't such a bad thing. Making the same mistakes over and over is what you want to avoid

WHAT'S IN THIS BOOK

Okay, time to tell you what this book contains. I've organized the book using a timeline metaphor. My assumption is that you are about to leap out into the unknown at a certain date. That day I refer to as Leap Day, and for that day to be as successful as possible, you have to prepare for it.

The first chapter, well, you're reading it now, and you're amazed and stunned at the brilliance so far, and you're shelling out your hard-earned bucks as we speak. It's the only chapter that doesn't fit the timeline—sorry, its designed to rope you in, to make the sale, close the deal, you know. Moving right along ...

The second chapter is called So You Wanna Be A Consultant? In it, I'll cover all the things you need to know and do before you make that big leap. It's all about focusing on what you want to do, setting goals, figuring out what your values are, and doing some initial research so you don't fall flat on your face. It also gives you some sure-fire techniques for setting your fees.

More to the point, this chapter is about what you shouldn't be doing. You shouldn't be hiring a lawyer to incorporate. You shouldn't be hiring a CPA to get your books in order. You definitely shouldn't be hiring a designer to work up comps for your logo. You don't have a paying customer yet, so you don't have a business. To have a business, you need to be in business.

Don't skip chapter 2! You have to set down a good foundation, particularly when it comes to your areas of focus and values. I'll talk more about this later, but rest assured that I wandered around like Moses and the Hebrews in the Sinai because I didn't have a really good idea of where I wanted to go or how I wanted to get there. Things are so much easier now, because I know what I stand for.

The third chapter, Leap Day, is all about the big day. You're leaving your job, striking out on your own, and all that good stuff you've been planning. What do you need on day one? Yes, there's some stuff in here about phone lines and promotional emails, but there's also some other goodies too.

The fourth chapter, First 30 Days, builds on the first day. In it you'll learn how to build a system that will help your marketing wheels turn. You'll learn how to pitch clients and write proposals. You'll learn how to identify good prospects from bad.

The fourth chapter, Hitting the 90 Day Mark, moves you into the next phase of your world-domination plan. Now it's time to do all those crazy things that everyone tells you to have before you start. Go ahead, hire a lawyer, hire a designer, get a logo. Happy now? Okay, now it's also time to explore some other things, fun things, like creating a teleseminar series, getting booked as a speaker, and writing articles in your area of expertise. I'll also talk about serving on the boards of non-profit organizations.

The sixth chapter, The Six Month Mark, is a time for assessment and simplification. Which clients are the most profitable? Which ones suck? Which projects fire you up, and which ones could you live without? It's time to fire the bottom 20% of your client base—the ones that cause 80% of your hassles and don't pay that well anyway. It's also time to consider activities that will grow and diversify your income without complicating your life.

The seventh chapter, One Year in Business, is all about diversifying and growing your business. Don't assume I'm going to tell you to hire a bunch of folks, either! Instead, I focus on making more money first, then growing the business with hired help.

Finally, in the Conclusion, I give you a bit of parting advice, point you to my web site, and tell you about some great books I've found on Amazon that will help you grow your business even more.

A Quick Warning/Disclaimer

At this point, I feel compelled to issue a little warning. It may not be needed, but please indulge me.

As you should know by now, if not from the title of this book, but what I've written so far, one thing should be painfully clear:

I'm not here to make you instantly rich.

What I'm going to show you will take some work on your part to pull off. It will also take time. Most of you will need a year in business to go through the whole program. I don't mean to imply that you won't see results for a whole year—most of you will see some traction within a few weeks, and certainly before you hit the six month mark.

However, I can't promise you that as a result of buying this book and following the advice contained within, no matter how brilliant, that you'll be like that guy in those inane commercials, who, decked out in his bathrobe, shines his Mercedes en route to picking up a fist full of checks from his mailbox.

But I can tell you this:

I'm here to make you an insanely happy, productive, and sought-after technical consultant.

You'll have your bad days, your worse days, and even some good days sprinkled in between. You'll have your sucky clients, your great clients, and the workaday clients too. But in the midst of all that stuff you can't control, I'm going to show you what you can control. I'm going to light the path that will take you from corporate wage-slave cubicle geek to self-employed ninja.

Let's get started.

CHAPTER 2: SO YOU WANNA BE A CONSULTANT?

So you wanna be a consultant, huh? Well, we're going to make you into one. We need to take a substantial detour though. It's important, so please don't skip ahead. When you emerge, you'll have a business plan in hand and a good handle on what you want to do, how you want to do it, and who you want to do it with. You'll also know exactly how much you want to charge, and best of all, how to react to changes in the marketplace.

I've front-loaded the process a bit, but only because there's a lot to cover as you race toward that day that you become a freelancer. If you're already out there on your own but floundering about, this is a good chance to take a deep breath and do a hard reset.

The primary goal of this chapter is to give you a clear idea of what you want to do, who your customer is, and how you want to operate. The secondary goal of this chapter is for you to realize that everything you do here can be changed. You're not some giant Fortune 100 company or some monolithic socialist government, creating action plans that have to be executed lock-step over the course of 3-5 years.

Let's face it—you can plan and plan and plan and plan, but at some point, the world is going to intrude on those little plans, so you'd better learn to be agile, adapting to your circumstances. In this chapter, we're going to lay down a baseline for future agility.

So keep an open mind, and prepare to do a bit of exploring.

Ready? Okay, let's go.

First, You Have to Sign Off on a Few More Things

I've already made you agree to one thing, and I hope that you were able to pass the little test in the introduction. Let's repeat that wonderful little assertion and put it here to remind you again:

My name is [insert name here] and I am a complete and total ninja bad-ass in [insert name of technical prowess here].

In other words, this journey toward becoming a consultant begins with a simple statement of self-faith and self-trust. With any luck, by the time you're finished with this book (and hopefully well before that point) you'll be able to say the above statement to anyone you meet and truly believe it in every part of your being.

Now it's time to make a few more assertions, but this time, they won't be so much about yourself, but how you're going to conduct yourself as a consultant. I've selected each of these very carefully; in fact, you could say that each of these statements represent some major quality I was lacking when I first started out. Each of these statements represents a little bit of hard-fought territory in my quest over the past seven years to get to the place I'm at now.

Used properly, these statements will help you make good decisions from this point on. You must agree to abide by them from here until you hang up your consultant's shingle. You won't always remember them, but every once in a while, if you ever get lost or turned around, they will get you back on track. Everything about the advice I give in the rest of this book comes from these simple statements.

I'll list the points first, and then go into some detail afterward. Here they are:

1. I will put the power of congruent behavior to work for me.
2. I will ask the marketplace what it wants.
3. I will act decisively.
4. I will set myself apart from others.

I will put the power of congruent behavior to work for me

Whenever I mention the power of congruent behavior in workshops, I usually get a lot of blank stares in response. Congruent behavior is probably the most simple concept you'll ever run across, but once you master it, it will give you a powerful bit of leverage over your entire life.

What is congruent behavior? Let's define what it means. Congruent comes from the Latin *congruere*, which means to "come together" or "agree." In geometry, triangles and other figures are congruent if they are isometric—roughly the same size and shape. In psychological terms, congruence means having a kind of rapport or agreement with yourself, perceived by others as certainty.

But let's get practical here for a minute. Congruent behavior for the consultant or freelancer means matching deeds to words and thoughts. You cannot think to yourself, "Self, you will be a successful bad-ass ninja consultant" and then proceed to sleep in until noon every day, working only two hours a day, not reading any books on topics that deepen your mastery, or not networking with people who can get you any work.

Similarly, if you want to become a best-selling author, you won't get there unless you actually sit down in front of a computer or typewriter (or pad of paper, like my beloved spouse) and start writing.

My experience has been that when people say things like, "I want to be a writer," what they really mean is, "I want to have written." They may want to be a consultant, but they don't want to do all the work that it requires to get there.

So the first thing you're going to do after asserting your bad-ass ninjaness, is put the power of congruent behavior to work for you. If you want something, you're going to speak, think, and act like you already have that thing, or at the very least, are working your butt off to get it.

If you want to be a freelance copywriter or technical writer, you're going to get up every day and write. More to the point, you're going to learn everything you can about writing effective headlines, about documenting software, about crafting effective landing pages. You're going to send out five emails every day to folks who could potentially hire you. You're going to spruce up your web site, adding portfolio items that show off your work.

If you want to be the best freelance JavaScript gunslinger out there, you're going to use every day to your advantage. You'll learn a new function every day. You'll talk to the agencies and others who could hire you. You'll post code snippets and samples on your favorite forums, and help others who need help. You'll build a reputation every day by posting on your blog and being part of the community. Not a day will go by without learning something new.

Furthermore, once you've leveraged the power of congruent behavior in your own person, you're going to extend it to the rest of your life. You're going to start identifying all those people in your life who are only there to grind, tear, or slow you down. You're going to talk to those people (if you like) and ask them to support you in your quest. If they can't do that, then you're sorry, but you'll have to limit contact with them.

Why? Because nobody needs that in their life, but especially not somebody trying to go out on their own. A colleague of mine ran a successful freelance practice for a long time. Married somebody with two kids from a previous marriage. The spouse was in graduate school and didn't have the time to contribute financially, so financial security was solely all on my colleague's shoulders.

The spouse had a big problem with the ups and downs, the natural financial rhythms if you will, of the freelance life. Every week was an exercise in panic, with all the dissonant bitching and complaining that comes with it. Money slow? Fret and moan, but never lift a finger to help, not even to just say, "Way to go, keep up the hard work!"

The spouse never contributed a dime in the five years they were together. Finally, my friend broke down, shut down the business, and wandered like a gypsy from one job to the next, never seeing even a glimpse of happiness.

At one point, realization set in, and my friend confronted the spouse with it, and surprise, surprise, ran into a wall of negativity and utter lack of support. Divorce followed, then a return to the freelance world, and lo and behold, a thriving career.

Now, am I telling you to just turn your life inside out? Of course not. But I am telling you that you can't possibly succeed if you don't get congruent, and sometimes that means getting some other things in your life (besides yourself) straightened out too. I have been extremely lucky in that I have the most supportive spouse in the world—she always pitches in, she always cheers me on, and she knows that the right word can boost me to success, while the wrong word at the wrong time might distract me from closing a badly-needed deal.

I'm not trying to sound like a fragile flower, but sometimes all you'll have out there is your will to keep fighting on for just one more day ... and so I'm just saying, get that straightened out in your mind and in your relationships before hand.

I will ask the marketplace what it wants

Most businesses fail because they run out of money. Either their funding runs out, the loan gets tapped out, or the customers don't show up in enough numbers to cover the expenses.

Over and over again, I've seen consultants and freelancers pack it in after six months or a year because they haven't found a market. They're selling the wrong product at the wrong time, to the wrong people, or at the wrong price. It's a pretty big problem, and like I said, it's not limited to the small guy—giant car manufacturers and airlines also make this blunder. I mean, the biggest blunder in recent memory ("New Coke") can be categorized as "D'oh, we didn't ask the market if it wanted this."

The difference between you and the Fortune 100 giant is that you only get one shot. You don't have several million dollars to throw onto the bonfire of corporate vanity while you wander around trying to find a buyer for your services. You need to make next month's mortgage. And the next month's mortgage after that. Oh, and you've got to set aside for your kid's college tuition, and maybe a little something for your own retirement.

A good friend of mine once told me over coffee at a midnight diner a very salient truth about money. "It's what makes life possible." So true. If you have some money coming in and some of it set aside, you think clearer. You feel okay about taking that vacation or pursuing that hobby. It's okay to take your spouse out to dinner or go see that movie.

Without the money coming in, life and work becomes a drag. You feel like you're always fighting upstream. Every month you bite your nails wondering if you're going to make enough to cover the bills. Frankly, if you're going to live like that, go back to the cubicle, where there's less stress!

The first step to avoiding catastrophe then, once your head is on straight (thanks to congruent behavior!) is to simply ask the marketplace what it wants. You don't always have to respond to every single thing it says it wants, but you won't get anywhere until you ask (and listen!). You will learn that at the very core of business is humility, in that you have to ask the customer what they want.

In this section, you'll learn a simplified method for doing that kind of assessment when you first start out, but you'll need to do it every once in a while to keep your bearings.

Let me give you an example, as the point is worth illustrating. When I first started out, the big problem I wanted to solve was to bring the power of content management to the little guy. I'd worked for Vignette and Cisco and had worked on some interesting projects involving content management. For those of you who don't know what this is, content management software helps companies update their web sites with little or no expertise required.

A good content management system removes all those technical bottlenecks that you normally see in an organization. You didn't need to know FTP, HTML, or anything else, and you didn't have to wait a week for an IT guy to come help you—you could just do it. This kind of technology could be a boon to marketing managers and practitioners world wide.

In 2001, when I started Triple Dog Dare Media, there were hardly any good content management products around. The ones that were out there just sucked, in my humble opinion. So I set out to build my own using PHP/mySQL. Over the years, I revised my software about a dozen times, building a rather good, functional, and modular system for small and medium businesses (and quite a few non-profits, too!).

I charged anywhere from $7,500 to $20,000 for this system, depending on the modules customers bought and how much customization they wanted. I didn't feel too threatened by the arrival of the Joomlas, Drupals, and other systems, because no matter what, installing and configuring those systems required an expert. We could handle those systems and still charge about the same amount for going with them.

Around 2006, things started to change. Why? Well, that was about the time that WordPress began adding more and more content management features to its blogging tools. We also saw the rise of the wikis, which made the technology more widespread. Suddenly, I didn't have to go in and give a long presentation about the value of content management, everyone already understood the value proposition. What they wanted to know is why should they go with what I'd built when they could use WordPress or MediaWiki for free.

So I shifted gears, seeing more value in being a consultant on content management, and did that for a while, and then I saw what the marketplace really wanted: yes, they wanted advice on how to get stuff out there, but what they really wanted, at the end of the day, was somebody to help them write the content that went *into* the content management system. I'd already written a few technical books and plenty of technical articles for Amazon and IBM DeveloperWorks, so this particular progression was easy.

Lesson learned from all this? You have to stay connected to your market, because things will change. If you don't ask the marketplace what it wants, it will leave you in the dust, and you'll wonder what happened to your business.

I will act decisively

I knew a guy once, a freelance database wunderkind. Guy was smart. Way smarter than I'll ever be, by miles and miles. Get him inside a database problem, and he was a total samurai. There wasn't anything he couldn't do in MySQL, PostGreSQL, Oracle, Informix, DB2, you name it. He'd forgotten more about databases than you or I will ever know. He was poised to make a bazillion dollars as a lone-gun consultant.

The problem was, he could never make a decision. He'd agonize over every single step in his business. He'd literally get analysis paralysis. Should he start a blog centered around his true love, tweaking databases? Well, let's take his buddy Tom out to lunch thirteen times in as many months to discuss it, noodle it, push the idea around. And in between, research the topic until his brain burned at night with visions of what could be. Watch as other lesser talents created their own blogs and downloadable white papers and gave talks at conferences and write articles and books.

Listen up folks, I'm going to say this about a million times in this book (and even if I don't, I say it about a million times a day to others, it seems). **It's okay to make a decision in**

**business, especially if you agree beforehand that it's okay
to change your mind once you get better information.**

If you decide to do a teleseminar series, find out what you
need to know and then DO IT. Just do that first one. You'll
learn a lot once you do, and given that new set of data, you'll
either continue doing it, or not. The best part? You'll get real
data from your audience and the market instead of subsisting
on the paltry dregs of your own half-baked thoughts,
delusions, and daydreams.

Sometimes, the world of freelancing is like driving an old-
fashioned car without power steering. Have you ever tried to
turn the wheels on a big, heavy, vintage 1950s vehicle (made
with heavy steel) that didn't have power steering? When
you're sitting on the side of the curb, trying to pull out into
traffic, it takes a heck of a lot of effort to turn the wheel, but
once you get going, it's pretty easy.

Same thing goes with your freelance business. All you need
is a bit of momentum and then driving the business becomes a
bit easier.

For those of you who are bound to misunderstand me, let
me take a second to be clear. I'm not telling you to drive your
business off a cliff. I'm just telling you to stop sitting on the
curb, trying to decide which way to go. Just pull into traffic
and make some decisions. All you have to know is that you're
going back home, or going to the grocery store.
Metaphorically speaking, if you have some goals for your
business (we're getting to that part here in a jiffy) and have
some values to guide you, you're not going to make
catastrophic decisions.

Here's another point. So what if you make a bad decision?
You're not ExxonMobil, or Apple, or Nike. You're not going to

spill a million barrels of oil into some unsuspecting Alaskan harbor. You're not going to piss off a bunch of customers by cutting the cost of your phone two months after release. No enterprising reporter is going to uncover your sweat shops in Indonesia.

You're just you. A freelancer. A lone-gun technical consultant. Believe me, hardly anyone will notice if you do make a mistake, and even if you do make a mistake that someone picks up on, it won't be anything major. Trust me.

(This game is a bit of a balance, you see. You've got to have enough ego that you would try consulting, but enough realism to realize that you're really not that important ... yet.)

I will set myself apart from others

One last assertion before we get to the good stuff.

With any luck, there are five million of you reading this book. In which case, please forward all mail to Aruba, where I've retired in style. Even if there aren't five million of you reading this book, there are probably at least that many reading some kind of book on starting a freelance business, and countless others already out there doing their thing without the benefit of a high-value, wisdom-packed book such as this.

Do a Google search for freelancers in your specialty, and you'll run across hundreds (if not thousands) toiling away in your city or region. Competition is out there, and all you are is fresh meat.

You know what? That's okay! You want competition. If nobody's doing X, then that should be a huge signal to you that there are problems with bringing X to the market. Either the buyers aren't interested, or the sellers can't figure out how to deliver X profitably.

The key, though, is to be able to carve out a little niche for yourself. You want to stand out, become memorable, be that guy or gal who is known for something. Why? Because having a unique brand position saves you a ton of time and money, and because you'll end up getting a ton of referrals from all those other guys who are supposedly the competition.

Listen, if you're reading this as someone with a technical background, you've probably not been exposed to the world of branding. If you have, you've probably cocked a skeptical eyebrow at the entire industry that has sprung up around the concept of branding.

Everywhere you look, there seem to be guys running around doing brand research, brand evangelism, brand stewardship, and yada-yada-yada. They give presentations, lead workshops, and run surveys. It's okay to feel a bit weird about it, and to feel like you'll never ever fully conquer what you need to know about branding. Relax—you only need to read two books on branding to get it. The rest aren't worth a damn.

Those two books are *The Brand Gap* and *Zag*, both by Marty Neumeier. They're both presented as white board discussions in print, with lots of visuals and hard-hitting bullets. To make a long story short, and to cut things down to what you need to know, branding is not just your logo or trademark, it's a person's **gut feeling** about a product, service, or other offering.

That's it in a nutshell. A brand is an instinct, a warm fuzzy, a bad fuzzy, whatever. Companies can try to buy their way toward a brand position, but they usually find a way to screw it up. Nationwide Insurance spent millions and millions to tell folks that "Nationwide is on your side."

Katrina hit, and Nationwide started rejecting claims left and right. Cue lots of media coverage of folks who have lost everything (including loved ones) trying to get a check out of Nationwide. Not gonna happen.

So, is Nationwide really on your side? Their slick, expensive ads and logos say so, but no, not really. Their brand reputation on the street says something else entirely.

Let me just say right here and now that you won't have the time, energy, or money to develop a brand the way the Madison Avenue gurus think it should be developed. Instead, you're going to build a brand the old-fashioned way, with hard work. You're going to make certain promises, then you're going to deliver on those promises, over and over and over again. You're going to build up your expertise and become known as the go-to guy for X.

Now your job is to define X, and make X doable. You may not be able to become the worldwide expert on JavaScript, but you could become the best JavaScript coder in Boise, Idaho. You may not be the best technical writer in Austin, TX, but you might be the go-to guy for writing technical case studies. Or the best technical writer on network security.

Get the idea? Focus makes things easier.

Here's something else that makes things easier: zagging when others zig. Marty Neumeier talks about this in his book *Zag*. You will find soon enough that most companies participate gleefully in Me-Too Marketing. They look at what all their competitors are doing and then do the exact same thing. Those guys have a trade show booth/white paper/podcast, well we better do those things too!

Time to zag. Stand out. Do something unexpected. Our brains are hardwired to notice something that's different, something that's moving. In a sea of Nordic blondes, the brunette or redhead stands out. A single red dot on a page full of grey dots jumps out, draws the eye.

You'll learn how to stand out in this book. For right now, remember the golden rule of differentiation: the more competition you have, the more focus you'll need in order to stay competitive.

Now it's time to get practical and work on that focus.

What Kind of Work Do You Want To Do?

The rest of this chapter is devoted to a singular purpose: creating a short (as in one page), succinct, hard-hitting, realistic business plan.

To get there, you need a focus, something that's a good fit. A good fit will mean a high level of comfort, an ease about your daily routine, and the right clients. The wrong fit could mean a more stressed work life involving the wrong kind of work for the wrong kind of client.

For some of you, finding a focus will be a no-brainer. You are probably currently working in corporateland as a technical writer, JavaScript coder, PHP expert, database wizard, information architect, technical analyst, copywriter, Ruby on Rails master, or what have you, and you want to translate what you do to the freelance world.

For others, this part of the process will be a bit harder. You're probably already doing some kind of technical job and hate it, maybe want to try something new. You're coders and want to become designers, or writers and want to be coders. For still others, you're working in a non-technical capacity and want to launch out into the world as a PHP programmer or HTML guru.

Something else you won't realize right now, and that's a very overlooked fact: the kind of work you enjoy doing changes as you get more experience. You might start out doing one thing (coder) but move into other areas (training or consulting), or move from one discipline (PHP) to another (Rails). All of that's okay, as long as you're aware of what you're doing.

For those of you in that first self-assured group, please keep reading, as something might come up that could shake you up and make you reconsider. For those who aren't quite sure, or who think they may be changing things up, here are a few rules of thumb to help you figure out a direction in your technical consulting career.

These rules of thumb are not meant to be the end-all, be-all rule to help you figure out your entire career, just some questions that will move the process along in case you're not sure what you want to do.

Are you a strategist or tactician?

Do you feel more comfortable leading teams, having the 10,000-foot view of things, and devising strategies? Or are you the expert doer, the guy in the technical weeds? Are you the general planning the D-Day invasion, or are you the seasoned sergeant crawling from sand dune to sand dune taking care of business? Another way of putting this: are you a big-picture person, or a detail person?

It's okay to be either, but there's nothing more frustrating than building a business that doesn't fit your personality.

When I first started out, I built a business that was all around coding and doing all the detail work. It wasn't a good fit. I'm a people person. I like to be with the customer, figuring out what they need, then responding to that need with product. I didn't like to be holed up in my little cave, coding until 3 a.m. The more time I spent cranking away at code, the less time I had to be with the customer. Whenever I had a chance to be with customers, I was simultaneously happy but quite cranky, because I had a hell of a long list of coding commitments to tackle ... which meant I didn't have time to be with the customer.

Once I realized this about myself, I shifted my business so I could do more people-oriented things: more workshops, more high-level consulting, more tasks (like assessments) that put me in contact with people.

Remember, nobody will hold it against you, whatever your choice might be. There's nothing intrinsically superior to being an architect or analyst, as opposed to a coder. Throw that old hierarchical thinking out. Nobody's gonna be better than you—you run your own show.

What people will pick up on is your energy and happiness level. You want to gravitate to where your comfort zone is, because that's more important than you know.

Let me make a small note before we go on. Just about every consulting project you will ever take on will have ample opportunities for assessment and implementation. Even as a grunt coder or copywriter, there were always plenty of chances for me to ask questions or take some time out to figure out important things like audience analysis or usability surveys. What I'm talking about in this section is your preferred working mode—some folks are naturally good at strategy and high-level thinking and disastrously inept at implementation, and vice versa.

Do you like to build from scratch or work with existing material?

Most technical projects take one of three paths:

- Build something from scratch.

- Buy something and install it without any customization (very rare).

- Buy something, install it, and customize or tailor it.

There are some folks who suffer from Not Invented Here Syndrome, meaning that they can't be involved in anything unless they do it all themselves. When I was first learning Perl a decade ago, I scrupulously avoided using any modules written by anyone else. I was going to figure it all out by myself, or so help me I'd just die trying. I would spend weeks and weeks figuring out different things even though I knew that someone else had already solved the problem.

I'm happy to say that I'm no longer that stupid—I regularly use all kinds of tools, utilities, add-ons, and the like, because I recognize that the customer wants a solution right now, and doesn't like the idea of advancing my education on their dime.

You've got to find the right fit for your career. You'll soon find out that there are thousands of little microniches that involve coding modules for one kind of business application, and that there are people who spend relatively large periods of their career just working in that niche. On the opposite end of that spectrum, there are those who spend their whole career just working on general problems, but always building from scratch.

Again, you'll find yourself moving from spot to spot, but knowing ahead of time what you feel the most comfortable with will make your work life a lot better.

Are you more interested in human factors or infrastructure?

There are those who feel very comfortable around things like visual design, usability, and the outward look of things (CSS, HTML, JavaScript for example), and others who are more comfortable on what is usually deemed the back end— databases, business logic like PHP or Java, servers, and the like.

Even in the world of writing, there are those who feel the most comfortable with creating documents and those who support the writing—those people edit what others have written, build templates in FrameMaker, build CSS templates for online help, and write scripts that automate publication. Same goes with design—some folks spend all their time on interfaces, others on process design.

I mention this distinction between the "front end" and the "back end" because it is very common to see people who specialize in one area and not the other, and very rare to see anyone excel in both areas. For example, I've only met a handful of web developers who are really great at CSS and PHP. You usually meet someone who is a CSS master team up with a back-end developer when they work on a project.

Do you want to focus on one thing at a time, or have lots of irons in the fire?

Some consultants work best when they work with one client at a time. They charge higher fees, work exclusively, and focus on a task for several weeks or months. Some technical contractors work this way as well, doing their work on site for months and even years.

Other consultants find this approach boring, and instead go for the more kinetic approach. They have many irons in the fire, and are constantly working on new things. At any given time, I'm writing a book, drafting a few articles, doing research for a white paper or case study, and blogging. Some of my colleagues look at my schedule of commitments and think I'm nuts—they much prefer a slower work schedule.

Nothing wrong with either approach, but you have to find your own rhythm.

What are your values?

One more thing before we do some market research. I've already hinted at it above, and it continues in the long-running, oft-repeated theme behind this book: **you need to build the business you want to have.**

Part of that effort is your own value system. It's something I can't give you, but its something you really need to contemplate. Now, I know some of you are wondering what I'm talking about, or think that maybe I want you to get all moral or ethical on everyone.

You can do that if you like, but what I mean by values is very simple. I want you to know what you VALUE. Not what your spouse, parents, or friends value. Not what the market values (that's important too, but not right now). What **you** value.

If you can get a handle on what you value, then you'll have a better chance at actually building a consulting practice that makes sense. You'll attract the right clients, projects, employees, and partners. Having a good value system will keep you from wasting time.

This is all kind of mushy, so I'll illustrate with a story. When I was first starting out, I had a pretty good handle on what I wanted to do, but I had no clue what I stood for. As the old saying goes, if you don't stand for something, you'll fall for anything. Well, about six months after I started consulting, a good friend of mine got laid off and approached me about doing something together. My business was doing okay but it certainly wasn't going gangbusters, so I agreed to meet with her.

Her idea was pretty simple—help companies publish technical documentation. At the time, I was doing lots of content management work, and had spent quite a bit of time in the tech pubs arena, so I thought the idea had merit. We worked out some ideas and then I started to work toward this goal. Unfortunately, my friend decided to go off and do something else about three weeks later, then something else about three weeks after that, and two months later she was pursuing some other goal, and then a fourth idea distracted her about six months later.

Do I blame her for distracting me? No, not now I don't. She's what my wife calls an "idea hamster." You know the type of person I mean—they generate ideas all day long, but never get off the damn wheel and do stuff. She was the opposite of my friend the database expert who could never get *on* the wheel.

Truth is, I didn't have a good handle on what I wanted to do or what I stood for, so I just got sucked into her vortex and didn't escape until about three months later.

So values are important—if nothing else, they help you save time and money. If you have a set of values, you can evaluate opportunities against them to see if they're a right match. For example, if you're a committed Democrat, you'd be crazy to work on behalf of Republican candidate running for office, right? If you're an environmentalist vegetarian, you probably wouldn't want to work for a fast food chain that specializes in fatty beef burgers from cattle raised on clear-cut rain forests, right?

I'm not saying that you wouldn't accept a check from these folks if it meant making the mortgage payment, I'm saying that even under the best of times, working for someone at odds with your value system will be stressful. I'm betting that your outcomes might suck too, or at least, you won't be giving it your all.

Let me give you a sample list of my values, just to give you an idea. They come straight from my blog (http://blog.tripledogs.com) and are conveniently labeled "About You"—a section that tells prospects what we're looking for in a customer. In it you'll find more than enough hints as to what my values are.

A lot of web sites have an "about us" page, in which the company or organization goes on and on about how they were founded in 200x, their mission is Y, their goals are Z, and blah blah blah. This kind of thing is important, to be sure, but equally important is some kind of statement that tells you what we're looking for. Since we've been around for 6+ years, we've had the opportunity to work with all kinds of folks, and we've created a nice list of favorable qualities.

In other words, we like to work with the following kinds of people.

People with a sense of humor. No, we don't mean that you have to laugh at everything we say. And no, we don't mean you have to have our sense of humor. I tend to go for the Denis Leary meets Voltaire meets Don Rickles meets Shane Black type humor (wry/sarcastic/satirical/laugh at the pain kinda thing), which isn't everyone's cup of tea. I'm fully aware that I live in a society that finds Will Ferrell funny and I don't. Sorry. Can't do anything about that. But I digress. I'm just saying, have a sense of humor. I'll be doing a humor check at some point, because I believe that the funny bone is very close to the sentience bone.

People who are open to contrarian views. Mostly cuz we're a bit cheeky, non-PC, contrarian and un-normal. I mean, what would you expect from a firm named Triple Dog Dare Media? Not that you have to be a totally out there, risk-ignoring, flat-out crazy person willing to do anything at all, but we do want to challenge some of your expectations and mental models. It's good for the soul.

People who give us room to solve problems. Our problem-solving process is very heuristic, and is tied in with our learning style, which some have labeled as fearless. Listen, you can tell me about the problem all you want, and I'll certainly listen and ask questions, but I've got to wade in a bit to see what the issues are. That may mean just jumping in and swinging a cat around. Or it may mean just standing very still and watching the world go by for a bit. Rest assured, I have about 300 tools in my problem-solving toolbox, and 1 or 5 or 12 of them will help you.

People who really want to partner and collaborate. We don't have all the answers. We're not experts on your business. We need to ask you a bunch of questions. We need access to your experts, your data, your thoughts, your emotions, and your values. We tend to work in iterative cycles to achieve incremental perfection. If you can give us this, we can really drive a ton of results quickly and with high value.

People who know the difference between a real crisis and a manufactured crisis. I grew up in a war zone at the height of 1980s US foreign policy debacles. Bullets really did fly around, and people really did bleed. Everything else is trivia. Yes, I understand that your web site is down, and I will fix it as soon as I can, but please also understand that nobody is actually dying. And oh yeah, sometimes the site being down isn't anyone's fault, it may be bad hardware or a hacker in Finland trying to bring you down. This doesn't mean that we'll wait until tomorrow to get your site back up, just that you should have some perspective.

People who ask for clarification. My single biggest curse and gift is that I'm exceptionally good at pattern matching. I can extrapolate from A to Z after only seeing the sequence A B C. Translation: I can see the end at the beginning, and then I act and talk as though everyone also can see it too. Which means that I can take what appear to be huge leaps and zig-zag course corrections. If something looks weird to you, speak up. I'm trying to do a better job of explaining how I do my thing, but sometimes even I can't explain it.

People who need something done. Yes, I'm all for planning and thinking, but what we're really good at is execution. If you need something pushed out, I'm the guy who will do that, and keep doing that until the order comes in to stop the presses. One of our key values around here is tenacity. What does this mean for you? If you don't have a goal in mind, we'll help you formulate it, because without it, we're just not the right choice for you. We hate to wallow. I'd rather be moving in the wrong direction then just sit and spin my wheels.

People who actually listen. It's your dime, but if you're paying us to be the expert, how about putting some of our ideas into action? We're not saying that you should automatically operationalize every word that comes out of our mouths—of course not! We expect the give and take. But the whole paying us for advice and then not doing anything at all gets really old.

TIME FOR SOME MARKET RESEARCH

Now that you have some idea of what you want to do, it's time to validate what you love to do and your values with the marketplace. This is an extremely important step, as without a market, all you become is an out-of-business consultant.

A small word before we go any further. There are consultants out there who do nothing but market research for a living. You might be one of them. The professional uses elaborate surveys and methodologies that help them identify market segments and gauge demand. They create massively detailed implementation plans based on their findings.

You don't need that kind of detail. All you need is a way to figure out if what you're offering is feasible. Remember, it's very likely that what you have to offer is feasible, you're just trying to figure out how feasible.

Let me explain. You're not selling some kind of commodity, like a detergent or breakfast cereal. You're not going to be sitting up on a supermarket shelf next to all the other detergents. You are selling your expertise. You have a unique work history, a certain set of skills, and a network of friends and colleagues who can help you make your way in the world.

However, you will be joining a marketplace crowded with others who already do what you do. The key to actually figuring something out that's worthwhile is two-fold:

1. Target those who have purchased similar services
2. Find out what their purchasing experience was like.

The goal is pretty obvious: find out who the target market is, and find out what they liked and didn't like about their experience. One way to do this is with a phone survey of local businesses, but you can do the same thing with an email survey or asking a question on LinkedIn or other business-oriented social networking site. In the old days, I used a phone survey, but nowadays I use LinkedIn almost exclusively to do market research.

Using LinkedIn

If you don't use LinkedIn, start now. Build a profile and start connecting with others. I am an open networker (this means I promise to "not know you" if you ask to connect) and of this writing I'm reaching 400 contacts on LinkedIn. Just do a search for myerman and you'll find me—if you want to connect with me, send me an invite.

In any case, there's a section of LinkedIn called Answers. Members are free to ask questions on virtually any subject. You're going to ask the LinkedIn marketplace something that relates to your consulting niche. You want to find out if they buy your services, and what they liked or didn't like about the last person they worked with. Make sure that people understand you're gathering information, and not just peddling your wares.

Here's an example of an effective question and backup detail:

> *What are the top three things you liked/disliked about working with a freelance X?*
>
> *Clarification: I am starting out as a freelance X and am doing some preliminary market research. I want to find out what buyers of my services (specifically A, B, and C) have experienced in the past. What were things you really liked about working with people like me? What were things you didn't like?*

Your question will remain "live" on LinkedIn for about a week, and with any luck, you'll get a flood of responses in your email inbox. Many people will offer more than the requisite three things they liked or disliked. Others will point you to online resources.

By the way, having done some of this kind of research, I will guarantee you that some (or all) of the following will appear on the list of things that people don't like about working with a freelancer or consultant:

- Failure to communicate properly
- Failure to properly set expectations
- Failure to meet deadlines

Very rarely will you find someone who complains about fees, by the way, but we'll talk about money in an upcoming chapter.

Finding Out Who Writes the Check

While you're waiting for answers to your question, it's time to conduct other research. This time you're trying to find out everything you can about your target market, the person who writes the check for your services.

Find out everything you can—where they work, what their titles are, what kinds of projects they have to offer. Find out what they read, what conferences they attend. Read the same blogs and journals, read over the published agendas for the conferences. Absorb the language they use, the problems they talk about. You'll soon get a sense of what they consider to be hot buttons, problem issues. You'll use that stuff later to good effect.

Next, figure out where others just like you hang out. Does your profession have a professional organization? If so, is there a local chapter? How about a web site? Is there a roster of members available? Can you reach out to those people? If you can connect with folks, offer to take them out for coffee or lunch, and pick their brain about the local business climate. If you're brand new to the field, for example, and you don't know who your buyer is, then now is the chance to ask. Who do they normally work with? Who writes the checks? What are the big issues and problems that cause those people to hire a freelancer?

By the way, does the professional organization publish a salary guide for the local area? If so, can you get your hands on it? It's always helpful to know what the going rate is in your field—I mention it here just because it's an oft-overlooked part of your intelligence gathering.

While you're at it, find out if there are any networking opportunities available. Check your local business journal for upcoming events. Also check various web sites like meetup.com and upcoming.yahoo.com. In most mid- to large-size cities, there's something going on every night that you

FROM GEEK TO PEAK

could go to. You may be painfully shy, but networking is essential to your success.

Why? I'll be getting into networking later, but essentially, showing up to networking events establishes your physical presence. You aren't just an email address or voice on the end of a phone line. You're real. You brush your teeth and wear your underwear on the inside. You can do polite banter. You hand out business cards. You're real.

And more to the point, all your technical colleagues are sitting at home watching *Battlestar Galactica* reruns or playing *World of Warcraft*. That sounds harsh, I know, but I'm often told that I'm one of the few technical guys out on the networking circuit.

Nothing at this point should be dismissed. You never know what kind of riches hide in places nobody has bothered to look. If you're technical, it means you're analytical and process-oriented. Use these two attributes to your advantage. Dig. Figure out the buyer.

SETTING FEES

"How much should I charge?"

That's the question I get asked first when a wannabe or gonnabe consultant takes me to lunch. Sometimes we haven't even been seated and they're asking about setting fees.

There are plenty of places out there that offer advice on how high to set your fees, whether to charge by the hour, by the project, or by the day; and a host of calculations on overhead, taxes, travel expenses, and the like. I think those are all great, but all of them miss the most important points regarding fees.

Point number one is pretty simple, but it will change your outlook once you figure it out. That point is this: most people don't realize how expensive running a freelance business is, and **therefore don't charge enough**. For every dollar you bring in, expect 40 to 50 cents to never hit your wallet. That's right—it gets swallowed up in self-employment taxes, insurance, cell phone bills, gasoline, and meals.

You've probably been working for someone else your entire career, so you don't see all those other things. If you travel, the company picks up the tab for you. They withhold your taxes for you, put money in your retirement fund before you see it, and cover a big portion of your insurance.

Now that you're on your own, it's totally different. If the client work requires travel, you put the tickets on your credit card and get reimbursed net 30. When you get a check from the client, you end up taking out taxes twice—once as the employee, and again as the employer. It all adds up.

So yes, do all your little calculations: mortgage, bills, groceries, gas, insurance, play money (you gotta go see a movie once in a while!), retirement, etc. Then add a hefty cushion.

Point number two is equally simple, and it's this: the cash doesn't flow in as easily as you think it will. When you had that nice cushy job, you got paid twice a month no matter what. If you went on vacation, the checks keep coming. If you fell ill, you took leave and it didn't hurt your income. The money comes in like clockwork.

Out in the freelance world, you have to work hard to make it flow regularly. You might be busy as hell, with $10,000 owed you, but if those checks don't come in, you're still scrambling to pay the bills. And when times get a bit tough, companies find really creative ways to figure out how to slow down their payments by an extra 5, 10, 15, or 20 days just so they can meet their own obligations.

So two rules of thumb when it comes to fees:

1. No matter what number you come up with, add another 20-30%.
2. Always ask for a deposit of some kind before you start any project.

Doing both of these will straighten out that wild roller coaster ride a bit and make your life a bit more tolerable. The first will add more money to your bank account, the other will add money sooner, which will help you de-stress. It will also incidentally chase away all the losers who really just want to jerk you around—there's nothing that seals the deal like having earnest money on the table.

However, I know that approximately 90% of you won't follow that first bit of advice, and you'll end up going to market charging some ridiculously low hourly rate in the misguided hope that this will bring you a bunch of clients. To those of you who think that you can undermine my business (I currently charge $100+ an hour and $1000 a day and am nowhere near the top of the pay scales) by charging $30 an hour, please consider the following anecdote.

You're sitting at dinner with your spouse, and they suddenly keel over right there in the restaurant. They've had a heart attack. The ambulance arrives, and you rush to the emergency room. On the way, the emergency technicians revive and stabilize your loved one. When you arrive at the hospital, two heart surgeons are ready to go to work, but you can only choose one.

NIMBLE BOOKS LLC

The first is the top of his field. He charges $1000 an hour and has never had a patient die on him. He's performed 1000 heart surgeries in the past year, and is up on all the latest techniques. He's been a dedicated heart surgeon for the last 10 years.

The second guy is about the same age, but he's been a general practitioner for a long time and only recently switched to heart surgery as a focus. He's only done 20 surgeries and charges $200 an hour, but assures you that your spouse will be quite fine.

Now the question is, who are you going with?

Obviously, you don't really care about the money, so you're going to go with the first guy. (If you're the kind who would go with the second guy, please close this book now, put it down, and go away. I can't help you. Nobody can.)

Notice something about that analogy? It's rarely about the money. The only people that I've ever found who obsess about fees and the cost of stuff are people I don't want to work with. In fact, if I meet somebody who wants to chisel my fee down or wants special deals, I find ways to not do business with them.

Listen, the world is too full of great clients who want to achieve fantastic goals, and would love to work with you and your special blend of expertise and charisma. Don't waste your time with a bunch of losers who want to talk about money and what things cost. Believe me, if the problem is important enough, they'll find the budget.

Now. Despite my little anecdote and my exhortations about setting your rates too low, let me give you some practical advice about setting a proper rate. This won't involve anything silly like calling up five people in your area who do what you do and averaging what they charge (they'll probably lie to you anyway) or using a salary survey as your sole source of intelligence (people lie on those too).

No, do what I did one day when I was miserably stuck in $50/hour land with no way of making enough profit to get ahead. I went to a networking event and decided on a rash course of action: every time I met with someone new I would add $10 to my hourly rate. I would stop raising my rate only if two people in a row blanched at my fees.

I started the night by telling the first person I met that I charged $50 an hour. I should have said $60, but I was chicken. The second person I met got $60, and the third person got $70. By this point I was sweating bullets, but nobody was fainting away. The next person got $75/hour (I was freaking out a bit) and then the event ended and I went home.

So I decided on $75/hour. I felt good. I'd raised my fees by 50% overnight! About two days later I got a call from a lady in Canada who was looking for a technical writer to help with some marketing brochures for a materials science company (they made some kind of space-age polymer for the space station or something). We talked for quite a bit about the parameters of the project and she was ready to send me some information to look over when she asked me how much I charged.

With confidence, I piped up and said, "$75 an hour."

She got really quiet for about five infinitely long seconds, and the whole time I thought, "Oh man, I've blown it, I totally went over her budget, she's probably fainted dead away over the phone."

I was about to lower my rate (I really wanted the work) when she cleared her throat and said, "Well, I can see you don't know what you're doing. All of our freelancers charge a minimum of $150 an hour in this field of specialty. I don't think we can use you."

And that was it. We said our farewells and shortly after I went ahead and raised my fees to $85 and then to $100 an hour.

What about existing clients? How did they take the rate change? Well, let me tell you, I had this entire plan worked out to introduce the new fees to legacy clients (most of them were at $50/hour and here I was jumping up to $75 or more). I had this whole graduated schedule worked out, and it was painfully complex and my wife (who was doing the books) just hated it.

So behind my back, she just switched everyone over to the new rate schedule. Overnight.

We lost two clients (who were a pain in the ass regardless of what we charged) and everyone else just paid the new rate without so much as a peep. One of my clients called to say that it was about time I'd raised my rates, they'd been on the old rate schedule for a long time and wondered when the increase would come.

Do you want to know why they didn't complain? Because as long as I delivered value and demonstrated expertise, my fees didn't matter.

In fact, there's a paradoxical effect going on here, and it takes a bit to sink in, but it will. Just like you wouldn't hire a $200/hour doctor over a $1000/hour surgeon if it's your spouse on the line, folks tend to judge consultants by their fee structure. If you're below $70/hour, you're viewed more as a mechanic or plumber. Start getting up to $100+ an hour, and you're viewed as a professional advisor—accountant or attorney.

There really is no limit to the pay scales, by the way. I know a guy who charges $600 an hour for custom 3-D programming work, and another gal who makes $250 an hour (plus a steady royalty on sales) for online copywriting.

The other part of this that won't make sense to you until it happens (hence the paradoxical part) is this: the clients you'll have the most trouble with are the ones you charge the least. I've seen it time and again. The big-money clients who pay their bills on time and are a joy to work with need no hand holding. The other guys, the ones who have negotiated your fee down to a song, those are the guys who are a pain in the ass the whole way.

I guess what I'm saying is, you have two possible paths before you. The first involves miserable clients and fees that don't offer a whisper of profit, and hence, tons of stress as you eke out an existence. The second path leads to high-profit engagements, fantastic clients, and a fruitful career.

It's your choice!

WRITING A BUSINESS PLAN

Now that you've done all this thinking, planning, and research, it's time to put something down on paper. It's time for a business plan, but relax, this isn't going to be like any business plan you've heard of. Listen, there are thousands of business books out there that implore you to put together a comprehensive business plan full of market research and graphs and financials.

I'm not knocking that approach. A comprehensive business plan is appropriate if you need to rent a space, buy inventory, and require lots of money for operations and marketing.

However, you're just a single person, a lone-gun consultant or freelancer. It's likely that you'll be working out of a spare bedroom, do most of your work on a laptop, and have little other overhead.

So what I'm asking you to do is complete a one-page business plan, no more. Why one page? Because most of the time, a business plan is something you write once and then stick on the shelf for months (or years) at a time. It's something that gets looked at only when the business goes off the rails, and serves no other useful purpose.

What you want is one sheet of paper that contains the essence of your business—what it is you do, who your customers are, what your plan is to make money. You want it on one page because you want it to be functional—if you need to look at it, it's right there on one page. It's not scary or inaccessible. You also want it to be easy to update. You want to be nimble in your approach, and it starts right here, with an agile business plan.

So what does your one-page business plan look like? Well, that's easy, really. All you need on your business plan are four questions, and the answers to those four questions.

What are the questions? Here they are:

1. What do I do?
2. Who writes the checks?
3. How do I reach them?
4. What are my goals?

What do I do?

You have to define for yourself, in one sentence, what it is you do. My suggestion is that you answer this question with the assertion that opened this book. "What do I do? Well, I'm a total bad-ass ninja in technical writing, thank you very much."

But putting it down in one sentence isn't enough. You will also need to add a few more sentences that delve into the benefits of what you do. This will come to you from time spent figuring out the kind of work you like to do. For example:

> *I'm a total bad-ass ninja in technical writing. I write install guides, user guides, support documentation, and support notes that save companies money. Instead of calling technical support, users simply refer to my world-class documentation to solve their problems. Instead of floundering and wasting time, users become and stay productive because of my mad documentation skills.*

It's okay to get sassy here, by the way. Nobody else but you is going to read it. And so what if they did? This is for you, and you alone.

Who writes the checks?

So you've defined what it is you do, now it's time to put all that market research into play. It doesn't matter what you want to do, there's gotta be someone out there who will pay you to do it. You're not running some kind of charity. You have to live—and that means making mortgage payments, car payments, tuition payments, groceries, you name it.

In your business plan, you have to identify the person who writes the checks. If you've done your market research, you've collected quite a bit of data about hot button issues, potential customers, and the like. Of all those people who are potential target markets, you need to focus on that check writer. No one else.

The guy who writes the checks will almost always be the road to success. Don't waste your time with other people. It's a common mistake, and I'm going to keep you from making it. If the person who writes the checks is the CIO, then talk to the CIO. Don't market to the line manager. The line manager's job is to save the company money, and if he has to chisel you out of five thousand dollars to achieve that goal, he'll do it.

Not the CIO. His or her job is to meet strategic corporate objectives. If you have the solution, then he or she will pay. Let me repeat my assertion—don't waste time on the people who aren't writing the checks. They may be champions in the process, they may be the ones who you report to when you're doing the work, but to get in the door, you have to get the attention of the guy writing the check.

Here's another short cut for the beginner: most of your customers will either be middlemen or brokers (like advertising agencies or big government contractors who hire other subcontractors like you) or the end customer (like corporate clients or government agencies). When you first start out, you'll have a mix of end customers and middlemen that you'll work with, with a lot more middlemen if experience is any guide. As you build your customer base and network, you'll end up working with more end customers directly. At the beginning, you might be pitching the account manager or project manager at an agency, who then hooks you up with an end customer. Just so you know.

Write those people down now, and take the time to establish what their hot button issues are. To continue our technical writer example:

> *The person who writes the check is usually the VP of Engineering or the Manager of Technical Publications. These persons feel the most heat during a software release, and understand the consequences of good (or bad) documentation. The Tech Pubs Manager is almost always understaffed, and the Engineering VP is always trying to get the software out on time and on budget.*

How do I reach them?

Knowing who your target market is makes no difference if you don't reach out to them in an effective way. You have to show up where they're at to deliver your message; otherwise, you're just wasting your breath. In this regard, what you think you know about marketing is going to be all wrong, if experience is any guide. This isn't your fault, but it will hurt you if you don't wise up.

You've likely spent your whole life literally steeped in advertising. You've seen ads on TV, heard them on the radio, skipped over them while reading your favorite magazines, and ignored them on your favorite sites. Only recently have we been given those glorious tools like DVRs, adblockers, and satellite radio that allow us to ingest advertising-free content.

However, all of this steeping has locked most of our brains into a very simple outlook on marketing. It goes something like this:

Advertising = Marketing

Wrong. Advertising is part of marketing. The most expensive part of marketing. And most likely the least effective part of marketing, if you're a freelancer or consultant.

There's lots of other ways to reach your target market that don't involve advertising. For example, find out what trade journals, blogs, and sites they read on a regular basis. Write an article and publish it in those places. Give a talk at an organization in which they're active. Show up at the networking events they frequent. Get to know the people in their circle of acquaintances and colleagues. All of these things should be clear from your market research.

Let's continue our example:

> *I will bring myself to their attention by creating and maintaining a solid LinkedIn profile, by publishing articles in my expertise area on technical blogs and journals, and by networking at X, Y, and Z events. By the end of the summer, I want to have an e-book available for download on my site. I will also build an email subscriber list for my own newsletter, which will contain articles of interest to my target audience.*

Don't despair if you don't have any ideas for marketing yourself yet. You'll learn a number of effective techniques in this book that you can implement immediately--and they won't cost you anything.

What are my goals?

The last part of your business plan is where you set down your goals. Yes, you need to write down how much you want to make every year, but believe me, you also want to write down a few other goals, too. Like maybe you want to take a vacation in X spot, or you want to enjoy Y hobby, or set aside

$10,000 in savings, or have enough time for family things. You just can't work, work, work all the time. Believe me—I spent the first four years working 100 hour weeks without a break (except for occasional weekends) and then I crashed and burned.

These goals are mutable, by the way—you'll probably change this part of your plan often as you move forward. Last month's desire to drive a Ferrari will seem silly in the light of new activities or desires. That's okay. You can change your mind. Just write it down...it's the first step toward achieving what you want.

> *My financial goal is $100,000 a year. I also want to take a real vacation with my family— take a week off, go someplace nice, really unplug.*

CHAPTER 3: LAUNCH DAY

Now you sit with a much better idea of what you want to do, and you've got a one-page business plan that summarizes who you are and what you do, who your target market is and how to reach them, and some goals for yourself.

Now what?

Well, it's time to prepare for the Day of Judgment, the day you will step out and become a freelancer, either full-time or part-time. Did you hear the thunderclap when I mentioned that fateful day? No? Let me say it again. The Day of Judgment. Hey, that's really fun to say ... but I didn't hear the thunderclap. Nor did I hear any ominous music, bells, or anything else.

That's because in most cases, your launch day will go by unnoticed by most of the planet. Sorry to have to break it to you. Again, you're not Apple, Nike, or some other international superstar brand.

However, that doesn't mean you have to just slide toward that inevitable day you start freelancing and just hope something happens. No, that's just not my style, and it shouldn't be your style either. You're standing there with a business plan in your hand, a fire in your belly, and a day marked on your calendar.

Now all you have to do is get ready for launch day, and that's what this section will help you with.

First, how do you know what date to set? Sometimes, you won't get any warning. Your manager will walk into your office and announce that half the company (including you) is being laid off, have a great life and sayonara. Other times, you get the luxury of deciding for yourself what day you're leaving your safe, comfy job. Still others do a whole bunch of moonlighting first, building a business slowly over time while they hold down a steady job.

No matter what category you fall in, this chapter is designed to get you going within 72 hours in case of emergency. Everything in this chapter can be dragged out for weeks and weeks if you like, but 72 hours (a long weekend) is usually what you need in order to get your act together so you're ready for a new business launch.

You'll notice a couple of things are missing from the discussion. I'm making no bones about the fact that you SHOULD NOT go out and order business cards, hire a designer to make a snazzy logo, call a CPA or attorney to get incorporation papers started, or shop around for some swanky office space downtown.

All of that is going to wait until you actually get some customers. Believe me, nobody will notice at first that you don't have any of those things. I've only been asked once in seven years if I had incorporated my business, and that was coming from a guy who really wanted to know if I could refer a good attorney his way.

So, without further ado, let's take the 72 hour tour.

SET UP A GOOD WORKING ENVIRONMENT

Ten or fifteen years ago, every discussion of setting up a home office always came with this "hush-hush" air. Nobody who worked at home wanted the secret to get out—I guess everyone thought that home workers just sat around in their pajamas all day.

Maybe they do, but I don't, and neither do any of the home-based consultants and freelancers I know. I mention this only because you're just starting out, and that means you need to set up a home office—going out and renting an expensive office is something you just don't need right now. Remember, first we need to get a few customers and then we can start spending money. Having a fancy office isn't going to help you with new customer acquisition, believe me.

So let's take stock and get a basic work environment set up. We'll have plenty of time to get the details sorted out later. Remember, we've got 72 hours.

Do you have a spare bedroom with a door? That's the ideal. The door is the most important part. You'll want to close your door to keep out dogs, kids, and the bored friend or spouse who thinks, "Hey, he's just sitting there not doing anything, maybe I can talk to him." It's also good to be able to close the door to make phone calls in private and relative quiet (I have a Yorkie who loves to bark, so quiet is always important).

Having a separate room is also important when considering the psychological and tax-based issues surrounding home office work. By having a separate room, you send a clear signal to everyone that when you enter that room, play time is over—you are working. If you just use this room for business, then you might be able to get a tax break (please talk to your accountant about that, but not now! Remember, the clock is ticking!)

If you don't have a spare room, pick a corner of a room farthest away from major activity centers in your home. Don't pick a place close to the kitchen, laundry, living room (with its distracting TV) or master bedroom (if you have to work late, this gets awkward; ditto if you do any video conferencing).

If you don't have a spare corner in an isolated part of the house, I hope you have a laptop, because you'll be moving around a bit—out to the balcony or porch, your living room, maybe a local coffee house.

The next important thing is a good chair. You're going to be sitting in it a lot, so please get a good one—the best money can buy. If funds are tight, at least get something with a cushion for your derriere and the small of your back. Hopefully it also adjusts up and down, because it has to interface nicely with your desk.

The desk can be anything, really. The most important part for me is that it be at the right height and that it offer plenty of open space because I tend to pile things here and there as I work on stuff. You'll have other requirements, I'm sure. I picked up a good second hand desk for $20 at a scratch and dent store. Another guy I know uses a card table. Still another uses an old door set up on glass blocks.

Next, make sure that you have a good light on your desk— I like the full-spectrum lights because they provide better visibility and don't mess with colors and such. The idea is that they closely replicate natural sunlight. Good light gives your eyes a break, and you need your peepers in top condition.

That's it—that's all you need right now in terms of office stuff. Later on, you'll pick up a filing cabinet, maybe a shredder, but there's time enough for all that after the magic 72 hour clock runs out.

Now, I'm assuming that you have either a desktop or laptop computer in your possession, along with some kind of broadband connection to the Internet (cable, DSL, etc). If you don't, run (do not walk) to your local computer store (I'm an Apple guy, so I haunt the Apple Store regularly) and get something. Since you'll be traveling some (even if just locally) it's smart to get a laptop, but some folks just can't work on one, and need a desktop. Either way, get the best, most powerful machine money can buy. You just can't live as a technical consultant without one, and I mention it only because there is a slight chance that someone reading this might be without one.

Here's another assumption—you have some kind of cell phone or smartphone. If you don't, go get one. Again, I'm an Apple guy, so I have an iPhone, giving me maps for when I get lost (frequently), email send/receive, web browsing, instant messaging, and all kinds of other features besides being able to make and take calls.

You have plenty of time later to decide if you want a dedicated phone line and/or a fax machine in your home office—these kind of lines can get expensive, and you'll probably find that use your cell phone and email more often.

Build a Web Site

The next thing you're going to do is find a good, cheap web site hosting company (I recommend ModWest at http://www.modwest.com). By cheap I mean paying $15/month or less and getting access to PHP, MySQL, and some kind of basic statistics package. Don't get suckered into buying your sister's friend's cousin's web hosting package for $100 a month, there's just too many good deals out there that will give you the moon for cheap.

First thing you do is set up a database (call it whatever you like) and write down the username, password, database server name, and database name—you'll need it later.

Next, secure a pair of domain names. The first should be your name, like BillSmith.com. If you have a common name, throw in your middle initial. Secure a second domain that summarizes the major benefit you provide to your clients. For example, FastCopywriting or FlawlessCoding might be good (if they're not already taken). If you're stumped, make the second domain tie into your main buyer and your benefit— MarketingManagersWantCopyFast, or somesuch. If you can't figure anything out like that, then come up with a domain name that is outrageous and unforgettable (that's how I came up with Triple Dog Dare Media, by the way).

You can buy domain names from places like GoDaddy (http://www.godaddy.com) at a pretty decent rate. There are other places as well. Don't fall for the places that charge $30 for a domain name, when they can be had for $8 a year. Don't get paralyzed with branding discussions at this point! You can add more domain names and/or change things around later.

Once you have your domains, point them both to the domain name servers at your hosting company, making one of them a domain alias for the other. For example, I have TripleDogDareMedia.com and TripleDogs.com—the second is merely an alias for the first (I got tired of spelling out TripleDogDareMedia.com over and over again).

Once you have all that in place, no need to sit on your duff while DNS propagates across the Internet. Nope, you're going to go to work.

Point your browser over to http://www.wordpress.org and download the latest copy of WordPress (version 2.6.2 at this writing). It takes about 10 minutes to download, depending on your connection.

Once you have it downloaded, open the folder and copy the config-sample.php file you see in there and make a new file called config.php. Enter the database server name, username, password, and database name that your hosting company gave you.

Upload the WordPress software into the root directory of your hosting plan using an FTP tool like FileZilla, Fetch, or CyberDuck. Once it's uploaded, point your browser to either the temporarily available address given to you by the hosting company, or the domain name you bought (if DNS has propagated).

WordPress will detect your config.php file, install the software in about 30 seconds, and now you have a shiny new blog all ready to go. WordPress will even set up a new admin account for you—write down that password, it's randomly generated!

Let me warn you—the resulting site will be a bit ugly, but don't worry, you'll fix all that in a little while. First, though, you need to put together some content. I know I'm moving fast, but man, that clock is ticking, so let's get the basics out of the way!

Log in to the admin area and click the Write tab, then the Pages subtab.

You need to have three or four pages, at minimum, to start out:

A home page, which you will use instead of showing blog posts (I'll show you how to change this in a minute). The home page should contain an opening headline (11 words max) that summarizes what you do. Follow this with three to four paragraphs of body copy that describes how you solve the problem(s) faced by your buyer.

An about us page, in which you describe who you are and what you do. Because you're just starting out, don't say things like "I'm just starting out" as this is code for "will work for cheap or even free if you press hard enough." Instead, talk about the many years of experience you have in your chosen industry.

A contact us page, in which you list every single way to get a hold of you. Email address (set up an inbox with the hosting company), cell phone, main phone, IM, Twitter feed, LinkedIn profile, mailing address (we'll set something up at a mail center soon), Skype username, and whatever else you use regularly to communicate.

Optionally, you could put together a **portfolio page**, in which you provide PDFs of articles you've written, images of designs you've made, or code snippets or libraries. You could also just provide screenshots of sites you've designed (always take a screenshot, as sites tend to change).

That's all you need right now in terms of pages. Click on the Settings tab and set the home page you created as your home page (under Reading sub-tab). Now you're free to blog about some topics of interest to your buyer, or you can install some widgets and a custom theme.

My choice is to create content. If you don't already have some topics in mind, go to a blogging search engine and search for certain keywords of importance to you and your buyer. You'll see a bunch of bloggers out there who are talking about these topics. Pick two or three of those that you really, really disagree with and then respond to them. Voila, you've got a quick start to your blog. This is called "riffing" by the way, and it doesn't need to be mean or nasty. I'll show you some other tips and tricks later on to give your blogging efforts further fortitude.

As for giving your site a nice look, just go to Google and search for "WordPress themes." Pick something you like, download it, and then use FTP to add the theme to the wp-content/themes folder. You can switch to the new theme in your admin dashboard by clicking on the Design tab and then clicking the Theme icon you wish to activate.

Once you have a theme loaded, feel free to fiddle with it to customize the look and feel—you can usually make whatever changes you want to the CSS or background images. If you feel a great deal of comfort with this kind of thing, knock yourself out. Otherwise, leave it alone as the plan is to make some money and then reinvest it back into your marketing.

As for plugins, there are literally thousands of great plugins out there to choose from. The first you need to do something about is Akismet, the finest anti-spam blog tool ever created. Click the Plugins tab on your admin tool and activate it. You will need to get a WordPress activation key to complete the process—this is a very simple operation involving registering for a free account at WordPress.com and asking for a key. Once you have the key, simply add it to the plugin.

There are lots of great plugins out there, from polls to newsletter subscription widgets and navigation widgets. My suggestion is that you install some kind of newsletter subscription widget right away, because you want to be able to capture visitors' information. Because you're just starting out, you probably won't need anything else right away, so try to keep good notes for the future. The good news is that it's very easy to install new widgets and add-ons.

There. In just an hour or two, you've got a basic web presence up and running. It probably won't win any awards, but it has all the things you need to get started.

SET UP A MAIL BOX OR SUITE

Okay, it's time to stretch your legs and leave that great little home office. You don't want to publish your home address to clients, prospects, and colleagues for any number of reasons, if only just to maintain privacy. Trust me on this—you don't want some client showing up at your house at 2pm on a Saturday wanting to discuss some code you wrote for him.

Find the nearest mailing center that lets you use a "suite" address (as opposed to a "PO box" which looks a bit cheesy) and go rent a box. My local UPS store (about 3 miles down the road) lets me rent a medium-sized mailbox for less than $200 a year. They also offer a bunch of other amenities that you will find indispensable:

- They accept and sign for all kinds of packages
- You can ship UPS letters and packages from there
- You can send certified mail there
- They can hold your mail if you go on vacation
- They can send and receive faxes
- They can make your copies (and even bind them)
- They can shred your documents for you

When you sign up, they'll ask for some photo ID and a list of everyone who is allowed to get mail there for you. You'll get some keys and a sheet of paper with your address on it—once you get back to the home office, put this address on your web site.

It's up to you whether you tell people that you've set this up. Some folks are still strangely leery of working with a consultant who isn't in a "real" office. I started out at home, then officed in four different locations around Austin before landing back in my home office and staying there. During the five years that I officed outside the home, I held exactly six meetings with clients at the office, and only had one client ask if I had an office. Most of my meetings occurred at the client offices, or neutral ground, like a Starbucks.

What this told me is that you really don't need an office— save the money you would otherwise spend on this meaningless status symbol and put it to good use elsewhere (like pumping up your retirement).

SEND OUT PROMOTIONAL EMAILS

By this point, the 72-hour clock has ticked down and you're just about ready to launch your new technical consulting career. There's only one thing left to do ... you're going to send out two quick emails. The first email announcement to all your friends, family members, and colleagues telling them what you're doing. The second promotional email will be to those folks in your target market, telling them what you can do for them.

Let's take them one at a time, as they're both important parts of the Launch Day strategy, and they both build on each other. It's important to set the right tone with each email. Along the way, you'll learn something about email marketing, which will become a great boon to you as you move your career forward.

Emailing Friends, Family, and Colleagues

Your first email is going to be targeted at anyone who knows you — friends, family, and colleagues. The goal of the email is very simple: tell them about your "new news" and describe what you do in a very easy-to-understand way. Tell them that you're about to set off on your own, and what your new contact information will be like. Don't directly ask this group for any business, but definitely refer them to your web site, and tell them that you are looking for specific opportunities.

The key to making this email succeed (90% of which will be received by the recipient and then filed away or trashed without comment) is to stay non-salesy in your approach and ultra-specific with the details. These people are probably not going to hire you personally (we're talking about former co-workers, maybe a few drinking buddies, old college mates, and your mom and dad here!) but each of these persons has connections to someone who might hire you, so you have to give them the right information in the right way.

In other words, treat this email as though it might end up being forwarded to someone else, because it very well may be. Striking a balance between personal and professional is key.

Here's an example:

From: Bill Smith

To: <list-of-undisclosed-recipients>

Subject: Announcing: Bill Smith, Freelance JavaScript Coder/Copywriter/Web Developer [you choose]

Friends, Family, and Colleagues,

Well, I've finally done it! After ten years in corporate America, and the last three talking everyone's ear off about going out on my own, I've decided to make the big move. Starting September 1, I will be working out of the house as a freelance [whatever].

I will be focusing my attention on A, B, and C. Most of my attention and focus for the first 30 days will be in getting the attention of [whomever], especially those who work at non-profits/small businesses/ad agencies [you choose]. If you know anyone like that in your personal network of friends and associates who needs help with A, B, or C, could you make an introduction? I would appreciate any and all connections as I get my business up and running.

Here is all of my contact information, so please update your address books:

Address: 123 Main Street, Suite 101, YourCity, YourState, 11111

Cell phone: 512.555.0101

Email: bill@example.com

Fax: 512.555.0100

Website: http://www.example.com

Thanks again for all your encouragement. Let's keep in touch. If you're ever free for lunch or want to do coffee, just let me know!

Sincerely,

Bill Smith

Emailing your Target Market

Your second email will target those who would buy your services. Instead of sending out a mass email, you're going to pick out five to ten folks who should know about your services and send them individual emails that very simply tells them who you are, what you do, how much you charge, and how to get a hold of you. Your subject line should address a problem or provide a benefit.

You will likely have three or four different emails that follow the same general pattern, but that are tweaked a bit to meet the needs of different target markets. For example, if you are an SEO consultant working directly with marketing managers and also with ad agencies, you will need two different emails for those two groups.

Remember when I mentioned that you'll usually have a mix of middlemen and end customer clients? The middlemen are those agencies and big contractors who hire specialist freelancers to help them on projects, and the end customers are those corporate, non-profit, and government clients that you work with directly. When you're first starting out, it's a bit hard to just walk into an end customer's office cold and get hired, but with middlemen, it's different. They've spent years making all the connections and setting up the projects—all you have to do is get your foot in the door and then get hired to work on a project.

Don't kid yourself. You won't get hired to help out on a million dollar project because of one email—it's just not going to happen. However, the process has to start somewhere, and a simple email that lays out the facts can get the ball rolling, especially if its professional, and individually sent to each recipient with a benefits-laden (or specialty focused) headline.

Here's an example:

From: Bill Smith

To: Jean Smith, Big Advertising Agency

Subject: Freelance Copywriter Specializing in White Papers and Case Studies

Dear Jean,

My name is Bill Smith and I'm a freelance copywriter. I specialize in writing white papers and case studies for corporate clients. I've been a copywriter for seven years, working on B2B accounts like Y and Z and for such technical software publishers like J and K.

My fees range from $500 for a one-page case study all the way up to $5000 for a 15-20 page white paper. I'm also available to help write technical articles, as I have a lot of experience documenting Web APIs. On my web site (listed below) is an online portfolio with PDF samples of my work.

I am available to work on projects starting September 1. If you want to get a hold of me to discuss my credentials or possible projects, here is my contact info.

Cell phone: 512.555.0101

Email: bill@example.com

Website: http://www.example.com

Address: 123 Main Street, Suite 101, YourCity, YourState, 11111

Fax: 512.555.0100

I look forward to hearing from you! If you're available for coffee or a quick meeting, let me know so we can get together.

Thanks so much,

Bill Smith

YOU ARE NOW READY FOR LAUNCH DAY

Send out your emails to get the word out about your new business. Take a deep breath, because the next step in this book—and your burgeoning career—is to put all your focus on the first 30 days.

Chapter 4: Welcome to Your First 30 Days in Business

It's your first day on the job! You go into your office, sit down in your chair, rearrange some papers on your desk, and grin from ear to ear as you check your email for the first time.

Congratulations, you're now a freelancer!

Okay, that's about all the time we have for pats on the back, it's time to get to work.

What are we doing now, you ask? Well, please notice that your email inbox is probably full of well-wishers, spam, and other personal notes, but no direct offers for work. Nor is your phone ringing off the hook. You might have a few people who are sniffing around thanks to your emails, but nothing solid yet. Don't worry; you're going to be okay.

In this chapter I'm going to show you how to build a marketing machine that will keep the work coming in at a steady pace. It's one of the most important things you can do right off the bat—if you don't, you'll follow the exact same path I did, which was to thrash around for many months doing odd jobs until I finally stumbled onto a process.

The main reason freelancers and consultants fail is the "porpoise" effect. Imagine in your mind's eye a porpoise diving deep to get food, swimming around and cavorting with his porpoise pals, and doing other porpoise things. (Hey, I'm not a porpoise-ologist, I'm just trying to draw an analogy here!)

The one thing that the porpoise can't do underwater is breathe, so it has to come up for air. While it is coming up for air, it can't do all those other things it needs to sustain life, like eating, hanging out with other porpoises at porpoise happy hour, and whatnot.

As a freelancer, you're just like the porpoise, except you don't have a dorsal blowhole. At first you'll be busy marketing yourself to get hired on. Once you have a project, you'll get so busy that you won't have time to market yourself, which means that you'll only start marketing again when you desperately need the work, starting the cycle all over again. Remember, you're a freelancer so you don't have a big support staff that can make cold calls, attend trade shows, and do other things on your marketing behalf while you're working.

There are those who do the porpoise routine for years and years, and make it look nice and effortless. For every successful porpoise, however, there are thousands of others who just plain burn out or run out of money—they go along great, fueled by enthusiasm and luck. Then one day, they finish a project right in the middle of a bad patch, and it takes three months to get hired for the next job, and by that time, all those jobs are snatched up by others who have better systems, and it's so long freelancing, hello again cubicle.

A good marketing system, like the one I'm going to show you, can give you the edge. While everyone else is doing the porpoise routine, furiously switching from doing the work to marketing themselves to get the work, I'm going to show you how to put the marketing (which you probably hate) on semi-autopilot so you can concentrate on doing the work (which is why you got into this game to begin with).

For a system to work, though, it has to be:

1. Simple enough to set up in a few days.
2. Easy enough to keep moving with minimal effort.
3. Simple enough to change immediately, if needed.
4. Cheap, cheap, cheap.

Wait, wait, wait! Doesn't marketing involve some kind of black magic voodoo that only the high priests of promotion understand? Doesn't it involve captivating your target market with a hypnotic gaze and tricking them into opening their wallets? Isn't marketing just a sleazeball routine to make money? Isn't becoming a good marketer some kind of sellout routine for those who should really be employing their technical gifts in some other way?

Well, some of my more technical friends say so, but I have a different take on the marketing thing. First of all, marketing is simply communicating your value to an extremely crowded and busy marketplace. Walk into any grocery store or market on the planet and you'll see what I mean. Everywhere you look are dozens of vendors selling the same thing—doesn't matter if their products sit on upright, well-lit shelves or dusty towels thrown down on the sidewalk.

What marketing does is give those products a fighting chance. In 21st century America, products are advertised on TV, written about on blogs and newspapers, discussed among friends, and lavished with multi-million dollar branding budgets. Walk into your average bazaar in Tunisia, and products are hawked by vendors using their own voices and waving limbs. At the end of the day, it's all the same except for scale and budgets.

All of this seemingly diverse marketing activity has one thing in common: it takes a lot of time and effort. Marketing yourself, you'll soon learn, is much more time-intensive than doing that thing you do. However, it's the marketing of yourself that is the key to success as a freelancer. Show me an expert coder without a marketing system and a mediocre coder with an excellent marketing system, and I'll show you a financially successful mediocre coder. This mere fact enrages a lot of technical folks, but please don't shoot the messenger for delivering the stark truth.

A system can solve the problem by giving you the necessary leverage you need to get the word out without requiring tons of time to implement...leaving all that time to actually do what you really love to do (writing, coding, designing, whatever). Those of you who have been following along and doing your homework also know that by setting up a system, something else happens too—the business starts to run itself after a fashion. You can go on vacation for a week and still have your marketing system working for you while you're gone, which means you don't have to start over every time you come back from a break!

What follows is simple: show the expert coder how to put together a system, and he'll beat the pants off the competition and still have plenty of time on his hands to be an expert coder.

STEP 1: BUILD CREDIBILITY AND VISIBILITY

There it was, my third year in business, and I was feeling pretty cocky about my success. I had a steady flow of 15-20 clients giving me all kinds of project work, I had an office downtown (okay, it was really a refurbished closet in an attic space), and life was good.

I didn't have a marketing system, though, and you could tell. I spent most of my days working long hours, then putting time in to marketing myself—going to networking events, sending out email newsletters, updating my blog, and other stuff, all of it at the spur of the moment. I didn't mind doing any of these things, but I sure was working hard and not seeing that much return on my investment. In other words, I was putting in 3-4 hours a day (minimum) on my marketing, but I wasn't seeing an appreciable increase in the work I was getting.

At some point, I decided that I would advertise. I hadn't done any advertising before, as I never had the kind of money to throw around. I'd saved up about three grand and was itching to put it to use. I called the local business journal to see if they could help me in my quest to grow my little business.

They were only too happy to oblige. They sent out a nice young lady (with an awful lot of pulchritude, as I recall) to talk me through all the options, discuss budgets, goals, and other things that had such a nice consultative ring to it. In the end, I decided to buy a quarter page ad in their annual book of lists. The book of lists is this oversized (8.5" x 14") book that lists the top 25 companies in different business categories.

That year, my little consulting group, Triple Dog Dare Media, had debuted on the list at number 24 on the Top 25 Web Developers list, so I figured buying an ad in the book would help solidify my exposure.

I also thought the ad buy was a great deal because the book stayed on the shelves for a whole year, being used as a valuable business resource by those who purchased it.

I signed the contract, and my three thousand dollars went into their bank account. I created the ad in Illustrator and sent it over. About a month later, the book came out, and I received my free copy so I could show all my friends how great I was for having an ad.

Over the course of the next 12 months, I received, by my count, about 100 calls based on that ad—about 10 of which came in the first week the book hit the shelves. Unfortunately, 90% of those calls (at least) were from other ad sales agents wanting to know if I'd like to buy ads in their publications. Of the remainder, half of them didn't understand the ad (I had put out an ad talking about web site content management, they wanted to know if I could design their site, which I really wasn't interested in doing) and the other half were from friends and associates who had seen the ad and felt compelled to call and chit-chat.

Amount of business from the ad over the course of those 12 months: zero dollars. At the beginning of the process, the arithmetic seemed so simple: if I could just sell one engagement (average ticket price of $7,500) I would more than double what it cost to put the ad out there. Foiled again.

There's one thing that's true here in Austin, and true no matter where you live and work on planet Earth: if you're a consultant or freelancer, you can't convince anyone to buy your services with an ad.

Why? Because advertising is primarily about visibility—about being seen or heard in that crowded marketplace. But visibility is only half the game—it's like showing up with a ball to the field, but what is the game we're playing? Showing up with a football to a baseball game gives you plenty of visibility, but to be credible, you need to show up with the right stuff.

And that's exactly what you need: credibility. But the extremely short nature of the ad format (30 seconds on TV or radio, small space in print or online) rarely gives you the chance to really be credible.

See, in order to have a viable marketing system, everything you do in the system must pump up your visibility and credibility at the same time. Nobody ever looked at an ad for a technical consultant and said, "Oh yeah, that's what I need—a content management system. I'm so stupid! Why didn't I think of that? Let me call right now!"

Whatever visibility that ad gave me did nothing in the credibility department. That's not advertising's fault, mind you—it is a poor vehicle for building credibility in this context (if you're selling running shoes or deodorant, you have something of a shot, but not technical services). So really, this was my fault for being duped.

Read everything that comes next through this very important prism—**you have to build credibility and raise visibility at the same time**. Go back and underline that phrase. If you don't remember anything else from this little book, remember that.

Achieving just one or the other leads to low yields and low returns. Ditto if you pull one off really well but the other only half-assed. You have to have both elements in play, and the results are synergistic—in other words, 1 + 1 will equal 3 or more.

So remember this first step as we go along. You're gonna want a system. But it isn't enough. You also need the system to do something useful.

Step 2: Turn Strangers into Prospects

People do business with people they know, like, and trust, usually in that order. When I first read that (forgive me if I don't remember where or when) I thought, "Nahhhhh, that's not right. People do business with the best qualified vendor."

Ha! That's when the education really began. Time and time again I lost bids to guys who were friends with the guy doing the hiring, or to guys who did the best job of schmoozing it up. It was frustrating, but at the same time, I didn't want to go the same route—in the long run, being the best party animal isn't the best way to build a lasting reputation.

If someone is going to hire you to solve a technical problem, which by its very nature is probably complex, maybe even so complex that's it tearing the heart out of their business, then they have to trust you. Stated another way, you have to have a certain amount of credibility in order for that trust to even evince itself.

In most cases, trust comes when you like someone. In some extreme cases this may not be true—for example, if you're in a burning building, you have to trust a complete stranger to save your behind. This stranger is a fireman, but he comes bursting on the scene with all kinds of trust-building credibility badges—uniform, axe, hose, and a bunch of other guys with the same accoutrements. You immediately like them because their symbols of office represent a brand that you find engaging—nothing like saving your bacon to build an instant friendship, huh?

Imagine for a second if some random guy just comes storming into your house in the middle of the night and tells you to get out because the place is on fire. What's worse, he's carrying a big axe but doesn't have on a uniform or oxygen tank or anything else. He's just a really urgent-sounding guy with an axe, shouting at you from the foot of your bed.

The house may genuinely be one fire, but you're probably going to call the cops. If you were in Texas, you'd probably shoot the guy 17 times and then call the cops. (I get to make macabre jokes about Texas because I live here, dammit.)

Meanwhile, your house is burning down.

The analogy fits, if you think about it. You can see that the client's house is burning down. You bust in with a cold call or unsolicited email to tell them about the fire, and they're going to have one of the following reactions:

- Yeah, right...whatever.
- Security! Get this guy out of here!
- Oh, thanks, I'll have my trusted guys look at that, we appreciate your concern.

In only rare cases will they actually be impressed enough to actually listen to what you have to say and then hire you. It's rare because you have little or no credibility with them.

So what's the solution? To get to a place where they trust you, they have to like you. To get to that place, they have to get to know you. To do that, you have to build a three-part system that will lead them to a place of trust and credibility.

What you need is a simple marketing system that attracts the attention of a complete stranger, gives them some essential piece of information in exchange for their contact information, which you then use to give them more and more information in different ways (podcast, teleseminar, workshop) and that leads to either a face-to-face meeting or a small-effort marketing campaign (like an email newsletter) to maintain the relationship.

Let's build a program like that, remembering to keep it simple so you can implement it immediately.

1. Go Back to Your Research

All successful marketing messages (actually, all successful messages period) are keyed to an audience. If you're going to build their trust, you have to know what they consider trustworthy. In most cases, as a technical consultant, the fastest route toward trustworthiness is to take an approach that informs, educates, and empowers the client to make good decisions—not just now, but in the future as well.

Don't worry that you're giving away the goods! Just follow along, trust me. (You should like me by now, right?)

Right now, you have a bunch of information about your possible customers thanks to the market research you did. You know something about their wants, needs, and desires. You've explored some hot button topics, the benefits that they're after, the problems they're facing. What you want to do is survey all of this data and try to pick out some patterns.

Let's say that you're a web developer who wants to help companies revamp their web sites for accessibility. You look through your notes and notice that a lot of companies that seek state and federal contracts are struggling with making their online materials accessible to the visually impaired. It's a big problem, considering that they could be winning many more millions of dollars in projects if they could just lick the problem.

If you've been following the program, you've already set up a web site with WordPress and sent out an introductory email to some folks you think might be buyers of your services. In this email and your web site you're probably already talking about some specific issues related to accessibility (you'd better have some blog posts on the topic, for instance) as opposed to just the general topic of "web development." (Remember: set yourself apart!)

What you're going to do now is implement a marketing campaign centered around revamping your site for accessibility. The goal of the campaign is get prospects to register for some bit of information, thereby giving you their name and email address which you can use later on to follow up with them.

This kind of campaign is called a lead generation campaign, by the way. That's a shout out to all the marketing geeks out there. Don't worry about the name, we'll just worry about making you an instant expert.

2. Create a Simple Tip Sheet

Next, create a one-page tip sheet that tells folks "How to Revamp Your Site for Accessibility" in six easy steps. Or take a slightly different tack, revealing the "Eight Things You Didn't Know About Accessibility." Or, better yet, go with the angle of "Seven Things You Can Do Today To Make Your Site Accessible."

Keep it to one page. Nobody has time to read a really long white paper, and besides, nobody knows who you are, remember? You're not Gartner or Forrester, you're just little old you. It's always better to create something meaningful and short—its easier for you to produce it, and easier for others to consume it (and share it with others).

Once you've written the piece (which should only take about 30 minutes!) give it a good edit, add your contact information in an About the Author section at the end (remember to keep it at one page, so single space it), and convert it to PDF.

3. Post the Tip Sheet to your Site

Using WordPress, upload the PDF to your blog. The easiest way to do this is to create a page in WordPress that is titled "Download a Free Tip Sheet on X." In one paragraph, describe the benefit people get from the tip sheet, and then add a simple form that captures their name and email address. Once they fill in that information, redirect them to the tip sheet for download.

4. Promote the Tip Sheet

Immediately post a news item on your blog that describes the problem of X (in this case, accessibility) and then link to the new tip sheet you posted. Do a little bit of research on all the bloggers who cover X and send them a personal note about the new tip sheet, pointing them to the blog post.

Then take the blog post and use it to craft an email to anyone you think might be interested in reading the tip sheet for themselves. Send that email out to your primary buyers. Once you have that done, contact every e-zine publisher you can think of via email to see if they would be interested in your tip sheet.

Instead of sending them the whole tip sheet though, you're going to concentrate on just one item from your tip sheet, using it as the groundwork for a single-issue piece that is 150-200 words long or so. You'll send that piece in to the e-zine publishers along with a link to the published tip sheet for those who want to get the rest of the story.

Once you do that, you'll write a slightly modified version of this article for PrWeb.com. PrWeb.com is a low-cost site that allows you to send out press releases to those who sign up to get targeted information. The only modification you need to make is to lightly focus on two bullets from the original tip sheet—the idea is to spread the idea about your talents without using the same content excessively.

Next, you'll post this same modified article at the various article marketing sites around the Web—that way your article will be picked up numerous times by all the other e-zine publishers and bloggers you didn't reach originally.

The goal is to pump up not only the number of incoming links to your site (thus boosting your overall Google PageRank and therefore your visibility in the search engines) but to get a bunch of folks who sign up for the tip sheet and therefore subscribe to your mailing list in the process.

5. Invite the Subscribers to a Follow Up Event

Every few days, check your subscriptions to see how many folks have registered for your free tip sheet. Invite those people to attend an exclusive, once-a-month FREE call with you where you discuss issues surrounding X. Make it a one-hour call on the same day every month (like the second Thursday or third Wednesday). Avoid Mondays and Fridays—you'll get next to no response.

You can quickly and easily set up teleseminars over at FreeConferenceCall.com, an amazing service that provides up to 90 lines for each call—all participants have to do is call a certain number (usually in 712 area code) and punch in an access code for the call. You punch in a different access code as the moderator and get access to admin features, like recording the call (this is crucial for ongoing marketing efforts).

Preparing for the call is straightforward—you can go it alone, talking in greater depth about the issues on the tip sheets and close with a Q&A session, or you can get an expert colleague to come on the "show" with you to discuss the issues that are relevant to the topic and audience. You can also do a bit of prep work, sending out a simple survey asking people what should be covered in the call as relates to topic X.

About three quarters of the way through the call, be sure to make a call to action—tell the listeners that the first five folks who send an email to your email address will get a free one-hour consultation with you. You can do this at the beginning of the show, of course, but don't do it too early, as it makes people think you're just trying to sell stuff. Don't do it at the very end, because lots of folks leave calls well before the "show" is over.

6. Market Accordingly

At the end of this first cycle, you now have three distinct categories of prospects:

1. Those who downloaded the tip sheet and took no further action.
2. Those who downloaded the tip sheet, then ended up at the teleseminar, then took no further action.
3. Those who downloaded the tip sheet, ended up in the teleseminar, and then signed up for the free consultation.

Of all these, group #3 is the closest to a sale. Immediately respond to those folks and set up your consultations. When you do your consultation, ask them what they want to talk about and then go through your process with them, dispensing advice, looking at stuff, and what have you. Don't be a sales animal here—give them value, but keep it under an hour.

In the last ten minutes, give them your pitch—in fact, this won't be such a scary thing, because you'll find that most of the people you deal with will ask you for the pitch, and it often won't happen in the last ten minutes. That's because you will have built up a lot of trust at this point.

(If you don't know how to pitch 'em, just hold on that's in the next part!)

What about groups 1 and 2? Should you just ignore them and move on? Of course not! Statistics tell us that only 5-10% of those who download a tip sheet or white paper are ready to buy right then and there. The rest, the other 90%, need further handling to get to a sale. It's probably way too early, or they're just testing the waters, or were curious about something. The key is to keep communicating with them in a cost-effective manner ... in other words, by using email and your blog. Later, I'll show you how to do this.

For now, you've set up a simple process that you can repeat like clockwork once a month. Think about the simple math of it: if you get 100 folks a month to download your tip sheet, maybe 10-15 might sign up for your teleseminar. Of those, 3-5 will sign up for your one-on-one free consultation. If you're any good, you'll be able to convert one of those into a paying customer.

7. Rinse and Repeat

Your job is to just keep doing this system until you grow really, really bored with it, and then do it some more, and then do it some more after that. Do not stop the process, ever, or your marketing will flounder.

If you feel the need to, change the content a bit by offering new tip sheets and new topics for teleseminars, or do the occasional webinar or live workshop as you get more money. You might even throw in an occasional video or screencast that shows you doing something or talking about something.

STEP 3: PITCHING CLIENTS

At some point, either because of your marketing system, or because you get a referral from a colleague or existing customer, or via your networking efforts, or just plain luck (you'll get the occasional random call from a client looking for your skills) you'll find yourself sitting in front of a client.

Because this is the section that deals with your first 30 days, and in those first 30 days we've been focused on building a marketing system, the goal is to get at least one client all the way through the process of downloading the tip sheet, attending the teleseminar, agreeing to the one-hour consultation, and then being amenable to your pitch.

First things first. Relax. No matter how much you warm them up (and that's exactly what this system is designed to do), you'll likely hear the word NO when you pitch a prospect. Just accept that. Even if they called you cold and you pitched them, experience tells us that in 80% of cases you'd end up with a big, fat NO when you finally pitch. The percentages won't be that high for those who go through a well-thought-out system, but a NO can still show up 50% of the time, and for the craziest reasons, hardly any of which are under your control.

For example, your pitch might be undermined by any of the following things:

- The person you're meeting with had a recent death in the family.

- The person you're dealing with just got their butt chewed by management (or spouse).

- You might have a stain on your tie from the hurried coffee you grabbed.

- Your pen might explode (or you might get a nosebleed, or your knee goes out, etc).

- Someone might pull the fire alarm in the middle of your pitch.

- The other guy you're competing with is this guy's first cousin's hairdresser's godson.

The list goes on and on and on. You can't control it all, so **RELAX** and focus on the things you can control, and those are:

1. You.
2. What you say.

You

You are going to show up to the client dressed appropriately for the situation. What is "appropriate"? That's easy. You're going to dress according to my tried and true Client + 1 policy. This is a simple policy that states that whatever the dress code is for the client, you're going to dress one level up.

Since most of you reading this are developers who hang out all day in ratty jeans and t-shirts with suggestive phrases on them, let me give you a few examples to help clarify things:

1. If they're wearing shorts, t-shirts, and sandals, you're going to wear a nice pair of khaki pants and a polo type shirt and nice brown shoes (guys and girls). In fact, never go below this standard of dress, no matter what. You can't go wrong there.
2. If they're in khakis and polos, you're going to do the same, but throw on a sports jacket if you're a

guy. Gals may want to step up to a more coordinated outfit instead of separates.

3. If they're in business suits and ties, you also wear a suit (for guys) or pantsuit (for gals). No need to go higher than this to tuxedo or formal-wear-land (hey, I have to say it) but you might need several levels of good clothes (Men's Wearhouse vs. Brooks Brothers vs. Armani) depending on how big time your clients are.

It's good to have a mix-and-match wardrobe to maximize your choices. I have one really good suit, plus 3-4 nice slacks (blue or black) with coordinating button-down shirts, and 3-4 trousers (khaki, black, olive green) with shirts to go with those. I can mix and match my shirts with suits, slacks, or trousers, and I have brown and black belts and shoes, plus socks that match the trousers. With just a dozen or so pieces, I have something like 40 combinations available to me.

The next thing you will do is show up five minutes early. Don't show up right on time or late, this will cast a pall over everything you do or say. Don't show up more than five minutes early either (ten minutes early is the maximum allowable) or they will just look at you like you're some kind of freak.

You will have hair combed, teeth brushed, and fingernails in good shape. If you are a nail biter, stop right now. Invest in a good manicure once every six months (especially for you guys, and no, I'm not kidding). A nice set of hands will give a good first impression and that impression is: you care about details.

One more thing—nothing looks worse than a guy dressed up nice with a pair of cruddy shoes on his feet. Keep your shoes clean, they really stand out if they're cruddy.

Take mints or gum with you. I prefer mints because then I don't end up looking like a cow chewing my cud.

If you're not naturally smiley (people always say that I'm scowling at them when all I'm doing is just thinking), learn to relax your face. Think positive thoughts, or a least, pleasant thoughts, while you wait or interact with folks.

Speaking of interacting, the first person you interact with will likely be the receptionist. Many a big deal has been lost because receptionists or assistants have been treated rudely or with disregard. Be just as nice to this person in the lobby as you would the CEO of the company.

Above all else, remember that you are not there hat in hand looking for a job. You are an expert who is meeting with the company in order to solve a problem that is costing them time, money, or market share. Act like it, and you'll start believing it.

If you are pitching the client over the phone, follow some of the same rules as above. Dress the part and you will act the part. Make sure that you call the number on time. If it is a conference call, call in a few minutes early. Be ready for small talk. Have all your notes ready so you can answer questions without having to fumble around. If you do start fumbling around, immediately go into "I need to look into that, can I get back to you" mode. Have a glass of water nearby in case you get hoarse or start coughing. Close the door to keep out kids, dogs, and outside noises.

Remember: you have to be credible and visible at the same time!

What You Say

Once you're with the client, a very strange thing will happen. The client will turn to you and say, "Why don't you tell us about yourself and what you can do for us." It's strange because you won't expect it, they've been trained to do it from years of association with advertising agencies, you won't see anything wrong with it at all, and its the worst thing you can do at this point in the conversation.

Lean in real close, because this is the only time I'm going to say this. If you want to lose the deal, go right ahead and start your little dog and pony show. If you've brought your laptop and have a slide presentation handy, then go for broke. You might as well, because pretty soon you **will be** broke, known around town as the best presenter to bring in when everyone needs a nice little afternoon show at corporate HQ.

I once had a guy who insisted that I give my presentation and kept frowning when I kept demurring. I'd learned through painful experience that my close ratio (in other words, the percentage of folks I'd get to sign a contract) would round to zero if I did my little presentation right off the bat, so I'd wisely stopped doing it. Finally, exasperated at my refusals, he said, "Well, Tom I have to say that I'm a bit thrown by this. The last guy who came in here, he did a real dog and pony show, and you're really disappointing me."

I turned to him and growled, "Sorry, Mr. X, at Triple Dog Dare Media we do not do dog and pony—we just do dog."

He laughed a bit and then let me do my thing.

And what is my thing? It's the one thing that will build credibility at this stage, and will set you apart from all the other yo-yos who come flying through there with their 60-

slide presentations about being the leading supplier of blah blah blah and God knows what.

Are you ready for it? You're going to turn to the client and say:

"How can I help you?"

That's it. Then listen really good, with a notepad in front of you, as they spill the beans. They will tell you everything. How this problem is happening, and how it leads to this, and it causes that. You will say nothing except, "Why do you think that is?" if you need clarification, or "Tell me more about that."

At some point, usually 30 minutes in, they will talk themselves out. At this point, you will summarize what you've heard, and then you will seek to get them to tell you what the problem is worth to them. Getting them to say out loud what the problem is costing will reduce barriers to the close every time. Let me give you an example.

I was once called in to consult with a local tech firm that had outsourced their technical writing to India. They were now proud owners of some atrociously written documentation that all the users ignored. This wasn't the fault of the folks in India—they just don't have the ability to write idiomatically correct American Technical English.

The problem was made worse by the fact that the documentation was supposed to guide the customers through a fairly intricate install and configuration. It was organized all wrong, because again, the poor bastards in India didn't have access to the software, so they were guessing, and guessing badly.

The result? Instead of using the documentation, the customers were calling the support center in Canada.

I asked how many folks were dedicated to just install and config problems. The answer was two full-time workers. I asked if they were both making $50K a year, and the answer was, "Yes, about."

"So," I said, "You're spending about $100,000 a year to deal with install and config issues. How about if I make it so that you only need one person part-time to deal with install and config issues? Would that be a reasonable goal?"

Now, saving $75,000 a year, that's a deal. Even someone who is deaf, dumb, and blind can see the value in saving 75% on costs. I offered to rewrite their documentation over the course of three months for $24,000, using my $8000 a month retainer as the basis. They would get a 3:1 return on investment. Sold!

I didn't have to do any razzamatazz. I didn't have to shoot my credibility to hell. All I did was show up, we discussed what the issues were, I sussed out the dollar figure associated with the issues, and I offered them incredible value after I got them to admit the pain point.

But I wasn't done yet ... now that we had built consensus around the key points, they needed something on paper. That's when I tell 'em about my one-page proposal.

Step 4: The One-Page Proposal

Whenever I mention the words "one page proposal," I always get people's attention. That's putting it lightly. Most of the VPs, managers, and business owners I talk to can't wait to see it. They can't believe that I can get everything we've talked about onto one page, but they can't wait to see it.

Why? Because these are super-busy people. You're not the only person they've talked to about this thing, believe me.

Sitting on their desk or in their email inboxes are seven other proposals, many of them with pages crammed with bloviated text, charts, graphs, and what not. They feature long and useless sections on the agency's history, lengthy bios of the players involved, and diagrams that describe the consultant's process workflow.

There's only thing that all that extra stuff does, and that is Hurt The Sale. The goal of everything you've been doing with your system is to efficiently build credibility and visibility at the same time. There's no point in being efficient all the way through the system and then blowing it with a giant, bloated proposal.

Nope. Remember, you want to stand out, and here's where you can leave a powerful lasting impression: with a one-page proposal that summarizes all the points at a glance, is extremely portable, and doesn't waste the prospect's time.

What goes in a one-page proposal? I never thought you'd ask.

1. A short, descriptive headline that summarizes what you're going to do for the client.
2. Add a subtitle if you think it's necessary to bolster your point.
3. A section on goals—what you are going to do for them.
4. A section called "current situation," in which you describe where they are at right now.
5. A section called "estimated fees and timelines," in which you mark out how long this will take and how much you think it will cost.
6. A section called "next action," in which you tell them exactly what to do—sign the agreement and fax it back, write you a deposit check, etc.

7. Remember to place your contact information in the footer.

Whoa, wait, is that all? Of course. That's all you need. What about the legal boilerplate junk? Don't worry about it. Why? Because any client worth his/her salt will make you sign a bunch of NDAs and other stuff before you even begin working with them. Believe me, you have plenty of time to develop your own. This is for right now, to land that first client. Simplicity is best.

Here's an example proposal that is short, sweet, and to the point. I used it to earn a $3000 fee for a very short blogging project at a technology incubator. Notice that each section contains only what needs to be said to move the proposal along. Remember, if you've done your job right, you've already built consensus—the proposal is just a document to seal the deal.

New Web Presence for XYZ

New look and feel, improved processes for better content.

Goals

Help XYZ build a new web presence by providing expertise with design, tools, and content strategy. Engagement includes installing and configuring WordPress and then showing XYZ principals how to create content for future growth independent of our consulting. The approach will be to help XYZ make good choices and then teach them how to "stay the course" with good content creation and management processes married to the tools in place.

Current Situation

XYZ Austin currently shares web space with all the other XYZ regional offices. XYZ Austin is looking for a more sophisticated look to help it stand out in the crowded brand space of North American companies. At the same time, XYZ requires some consulting to give its principals expertise on how to plan for, create, and manage quality content that will help keep its standing high among its primary stakeholder audiences (for example, North American companies that might want to do business with XYZ companies).

Estimated Fees

We wish to quote a project rate of $3000 for our entire involvement. Work items include:

Installing and configuring WordPress on current hosting provider (or new provider)

Helping XYZ pick out a suitable theme for WordPress

Working with XYZ to personalize that theme

Working with XYZ to identify modules and add-ons that will help them grow in the future (such as subscription widgets, event calendars, and podcasting tools)

Consulting with XYZ on how to develop an effective content strategy, editorial policies, and how to create quality web articles, blog posts, and news releases

Working with XYZ IT to redirect traffic to the new hosting solution

Timelines

From start to finish, we should have a new site live in 3-4 weeks. The biggest chunk of time will involve the design, as it is the most subjective part of the project. Other items that might take extra time are the actual writing of content items. The approach we are taking in this engagement is to teach XYZ "how to fish" instead of presenting XYZ with already caught fish--the goal is for XYZ to be largely independent once the project is finished.

Next Action

Client can authorize Triple Dog Dare Media to do this consulting work by signing this one-page proposal and faxing it back to us. FYI, we are a subchapter-S corporation, Triple Dog Dare Media, Inc. with Tax ID 74-xxxxxxxxx.

A QUICK NOTE ON NETWORKING

In your first 30 days, you'll be focusing a lot of your marketing attention on building a repeatable system. Following a good plan will improve your life and work, believe me—the alternative is to just swing away like a maniac at any old marketing gimmick, which will lead to lots of lost focus and money.

You'll notice one thing, though, in the midst of your first 30 days. If you have any colleagues or friends at all, you're going to get invitations to attend networking events. Networking is the new "in" thing, and everyone is doing it.

Every chance you get, you need to network, but only if the people at the event are in your target market (or can get you into the target market). Instead of taking business cards, you're going to make up a simple half-page flyer (that way you get two out of each 8.5 by 11 sheet) on heavy stock that tells people about your tip sheet.

The flyer should have a descriptive, benefits-laden headline that appeals to your target market (you might even re-use the headline from your landing page). Follow that with a quick description of the problem or issue, followed by a URL.

At the bottom, put all your contact information. If you want, put a picture of yourself on the thing as well, especially if you're even vaguely photogenic (which I'm not, but I'm saying—use it if you've got it). Be sure to get a business card from as many folks as you can, that way you can ask them to find out what they thought of the tip sheet.

At this stage of your career, this is way better than a tired business card.

Okay, One More Note: Project Histories

Whenever you land a job, be sure to write a project history and file it away. You'll be using these histories when you evaluate your situation at the six-month mark.

What's a project history? It's a short document (usually one page) that provides a brief synopsis of each project. It doesn't need to be super detailed, but it does need to convey whom you worked for, what you did for them, why you were hired (i.e., the objective or goal), and how you did the work. You might also want to jot down notes on how you interacted with the client, what you bid for the project, and whether you think you made a profit.

You might also want to jot down some notes on your interaction with the client, and if you'd consider the project a success—in other words, would you work for this client again?

The goal is not to be exhaustive, but to give you a memory boost. With any luck, you'll get so busy that you won't be able to keep the details of every single engagement in your head at once—and believe me, it only takes a few years for this to happen. Having some project histories written down will help you keep projects straight. This is good not only for historical or recordkeeping purposes (for instance, a client might call you six months later with another project and you can use the history to brush up on the last engagement), but can help you evaluate such important things as the accuracy of your estimates.

CHAPTER 5: YOUR FIRST 90 DAYS IN BUSINESS

Congratulations, if you're at this point, you've made it to day 31 in business, and you're motoring on to your first 90 days as a freelancer or consultant. With enough hard work, preparation, and chutzpah, you've put together a system that will serve you the rest of your freelancing career.

While your colleagues are out there struggling to stay in business, you'll just chug right along on your pre-laid track. Yes, you might see some of your friends and fellow consultants hit amazing home runs and score unbelievable deals, but don't get too distracted by all that. What you won't see is how many times they flail around, striking out when they should have gotten base hits.

Because you're just a beginner, all we want to do is get you a lot of base hits, because eventually, this will get you into a good scoring position not only for the current game, but lots of future games as well. I know that the baseball metaphor is getting a bit stretched, but every time I've opted for stressing the fundamentals, I've always come out ahead in the long run. Yes, I've given up certain jobs or projects that required me to lie or exaggerate to get the work, but I didn't want to work with those kinds of clients anyway. I've stuck to what I know, doing the things that establish a good, solid track record over time.

At this point, if you've been following the program, you should be well on your way to establishing yourself as a local expert. You've got a blog in which to share your thoughts and ideas, you've got at least one tip sheet, a monthly teleseminar, and a one-hour consultation. Chances are, you've got at least one proposal out there that's in serious medal contention.

Once you nail down that first client, it's time to expand your efforts to include all the things you bypassed as you got started. By the end of the 90-day period, you will have many of these in place:

- A set of business cards (and possibly your own logo).

- A more formal business structure (now it's time to incorporate).

- A series of blog articles published.

- A half-day workshop.

If you've got a paying customer at this point, then forge ahead with confidence. If you don't have one yet, don't worry—just keep on keeping on, as it will happen very soon. I've never seen any determined freelancer go more than 45 days without some work if they have a good system and the fortitude to stick things out.

TIME FOR THAT "ZERO ROI ACTIVITY"

One of the biggest mistakes beginners make is that they go all out doing things that cost them a lot of money but that don't bring in any revenue or other return on that investment. I classify business cards, logos, and incorporation (or whatever legal setup you want to have) under this rubric of "Zero ROI Activity."

Unfortunately, if you pick up just about any book on starting a business, what's the first thing they tell you to do? Go out and get business cards printed up! Hire a lawyer and incorporate! Hire a designer to make a logo! Rent a new office!

If you're following my system, you won't need any of that until you've actually landed a customer. Don't worry that you'll be in the middle of some pitch and the guy gets miffed if you don't have a business card. He wants a business card so he'll have your contact info—but you've already emailed him, right? You put your contact information on your signature file, right? Well, there's a time and place for everything, and now it's time to go make yourself happy with a new set of business cards.

Business Cards

As in all things, remember to stand out when you get some cards made up. Use a different material or size or paper thickness on your cards. For example, do a Google search on "eco-friendly cards" and you'll find all kinds of business card printers who are using vegetable parchment for paper (giving the cards a plastic, semi-transparent look and feel that is extremely sturdy) or who are printing small cards (1" by 2") on recycled paper.

Or you can change the card's orientation. For example, have the cards printed so that they have a portrait (as opposed to landscape) orientation. I did this from the beginning, and got some attention for it at every gathering. I also had my cards printed on really thick stock, and that gave us a substantial air. Also, it made it easier to get picked out of a random drawing from a bowl—you see where my priorities are? Not only do I get a prize, but the guy at the bowl says (in front of everyone), "Tom Myer from Triple Dog Dare Media (great name!), come on down!"

Other things you can do to stand out: put you photo on the back of the card, or have a different witty saying printed on the back. One guy I know puts a list of services on the back of his card. Another tells a little story using his cards—it's in five or six parts, and you end up getting just a piece of the story on each card. Another guy I know makes his cards look like a collectible baseball card.

FROM GEEK TO PEAK

I allowed all my employees and contractors to pick their own job titles. I was Top Dog. My wife Hope, who ran the back office, was BWTC. That always got folks. She'd explain without batting an eye that she was the Bitch With The Clipboard— BWTC, and they would laugh and laugh. I had a designer who chose the title Pixel Kitty, and a web developer with the title Deliverator (inspired by Stephenson's *Snow Crash,* no doubt).

I knew one guy who went so far as to create his own business cards by using recycled scraps from his home office— it fit, since he was an environmental consultant who helped companies get their recycling acts together. The point is, a business card doesn't have to be a staid, boring thing—have some fun with it.

Logos

Now, let's talk about your logo. Most of you won't need one, plain and simple. You'll be known as BKR Consulting (where BKR are your initials) or some play on your nickname (I played around with Myerman Interactive for a while, still might use it in the future) or last name (one guy I know tacked Industries to the end of his last name to come up with a funny, if slightly pretentious business name).

If you have a company name that involves your name or initials, do yourself a favor. Open up your favorite word processor and create a logo using just letters (technically, this is a logotype, I believe). Use a really heavy dark typeface like Helvetica Neue Bold or Arial Bold for the first part (your initials or name) and a lighter version of the same typeface (like Arial normal) for the second part. Maybe throw a bit of drop shadow under it and you're done:

myermaninteractive

There. You're done. I just saved you $500. (All of you reading this who are designers: get over yourselves! Business needs change from time to time. Business names change from time to time. There's always plenty of time to go back over this decision and "rebrand." From what I can tell, you'll want to do it in two years anyway, regardless of your involvement in the first effort. Yeah, I'm snarky. But you love me, don't you?)

If you've got a more creative name, like Triple Dog Dare Media or what have you, then you might need more help. Try to find a local designer who is just starting out. Take him or her out to lunch and offer to barter for a logo. You'll do something valuable (like write web copy, set up their database, whatever) in exchange for the logo. Believe me, you'll come out way ahead no matter what happens, because you'll likely use that logo for a long time.

Once you have a logo, put it on your web site, on any proposals, letterhead, you name it. Don't go all crazy on the expenses though. I didn't go all out on the "full paper system" (envelopes, letterhead, cards, note cards, and the like) until my fifth year in business, and I still had most of my original supplies two years later.

Incorporation

What I've said before about business cards and logos goes triple for such lawyerly stuff as incorporation. Put it off as long as possible, you really don't need it as bad as the "experts" seem to think you want it. Let that first customer write a check directly to you. Some would look at that and just blanch. "What about having the protective barrier of a corporation or partnership in case something goes wrong?"

Let me tell you something. I've been a corporation for 7 years, and in all that time I've never felt protected. The bank issues us a line of credit that is secured by my mortgage. If I default on that line of credit, do you think they'll take my house? You betcha.

Similarly, the clients know that I am the corporation—if they come after me, they'll eventually get to me. The protective shell of the corporation is just an illusion.

Again, you're not going to be Apple or ExxonMobil. So just move on for now. There's plenty of time to hire $200/hour lawyers and have them draft up stuff you could pull down from the Web or find in startup kits at OfficeMax. I'm not trying to crap on lawyers, but honestly, the last person you should get business advice from is a lawyer. They'll say no to everything. And they just can't rubber stamp a document, otherwise everyone will know that the gig is up.

Go ahead and ask your attorney, "Should I get out of bed this morning?"

The inevitable response: "No, stay in bed, you might slip and break your neck on the way to the bathroom."

So here's where I add my huge disclaimer. Don't take anything I've said in this section as gospel truth. I don't know your current situation. You may be working in a sector or industry that requires 500 layers of paperwork, certifications and God knows what. Do what is required to get the work. I don't want to get any calls in the middle of the night (or emails even) from folks who get into trouble and then blame me for their misfortune.

Let me spell it out again for all those in the cheap seats: do the minimum you have to do to get the job done, especially as it concerns all of this Zero ROI Activity. When you do have to finally do it, spend as little time, money, and effort on it. You'll thank yourself for putting it off and for not spending a fortune on this stuff.

CRANK UP THE BLOGGING

Blogging is one of those things that get people all worked up for some reason. Some take to it like a duck to water, others can't stand the thought of doing it. Well, guess what? If you want search engine traffic and others linking to you (**VISIBILITY**), if you want to show off your expertise (**CREDIBILITY**)—in short, if you want to be seen as a viable consultant—then you're going to blog regularly.

I know that I sometimes break this rule, especially when I get super busy with other deadlines (some of you may note some gaps in August 2008, May 2008, and other months— whenever I was closing in on a book deadline) but I have a good reason for missing out on the blogging—I was doing something to build my credibility and visibility even more. And to be fair, I am working on a couple of big articles that take more than just 20-30 minutes to whip up.

You, on the other hand, are in the first 90 days of your consulting life. You probably have a few clients by now, with a couple of projects keeping you somewhat busy. You have the time to blog—and in this section, I'm going to show you how to put things on autopilot so that you can keep ahead even during the busiest times.

The first thing you're going to do is go to Google Alerts and create news alerts for five to seven topics that are near and dear to your target market's heart. Ask for a daily digest of blogs, news releases, videos, everything that relate to your key words. Use a mixture of single keywords and keyword phrases—and be sure to put your search phrases in quotes to get higher relevancy.

In other words, don't just do a search on web accessibility, put it in as "web accessibility" to increase the accuracy of what you get.

The result will be a couple emails every day from Google, each jam-packed with links to stories, blog postings, and other content that relate to your express desires. If you're not too busy, review these every day at the slow part of your day. If you're getting busy, pick a quiet day to review the items you receive in the emails.

Not everything picked out by the alerts will be worth reading or writing about, but it will all feed the creative hopper, and it will keep you fairly informed on what's happening in your areas of interest. But what do you do with this information? You can use the alerts any number of ways to feed your blogging.

1. You can simply pick out interesting stories and then relink them from your blog, adding commentary or context as needed. This is especially useful if you want to be known as someone who aggregates other information sources.

2. You can summarize groups of related stories (picking out an industry angle or focusing on a vertical or region) and sussing out themes, trends, and other ideas that support your values.

3. You can "riff" on certain content, either agreeing or disagreeing, but always using it as a sounding board for your own viewpoint. Riffing is a time-honored tradition, and it doesn't have to involve negativity. You may profoundly disagree with someone else, but you can do it in a professional way.

4. You can create top 10 lists, like "Top Ten Posts on Blah For the Week of Foo." This is similar to the aggregation angle, but don't spend as much time on each item. The political bloggers do a great job of this whenever there's a presidential election—they do really good roundups of opinion pieces that many find helpful.

5. A close cousin to the Top 10 List of Links is the Top 10 List of Issues that uses links to support claims, theories, and viewpoints. This is a very effective way of creating "linkbait" (content that others want to link to and thus raises your visibility on Google). For example, you might have an article called "Eight Things You Didn't Know About Database Administration" and then list them off with a short bullet point each. At the end of each bullet point would be a link to another article that supports your claim or expands on it in some way. The links could be to other sites (best) or to other pieces you've written on the same site (not quite as good, but good for SEO).

To make things easier on yourself, pick one or two days of the week in which to blog, if you can't see yourself doing it every day. When you write, block out a few hours and just start creating blog entries. Try to crank out three or four of them, but don't publish them all at once. Instead, use the WordPress feature that allows you to set a future datestamp. Spread your pieces out over the following week, mixing morning and afternoon releases (you can do this quasi-randomly or timed to coincide with other events).

This way, you have time to review incoming information, write your pieces, and publish them—and it will look like you're a super-busy blogger who is on top of things.

Once you've got a handle on this process, you're going to go out and look for bloggers and other news sources that you enjoy reading—or who have something important to say in your industry or niche. Many of these folks will feature in your alerts. If they have an RSS feed, you're going to subscribe to them and read their posts regularly. You're going to follow the same process as you did with the Google alerts, responding to what others have said and posting your own thoughts for the world to see.

At some point (and this first 90-day period isn't that point) you're going to want to start thinking about writing something original and groundbreaking. We'll get to that, believe me. For right now, establish some smart patterns for digesting good information and then putting your own mark on things. Remember, there will be folks who only know 1% or 2% of what you know, and even the things that you hardly notice will be huge revelations to them.

I'm always shocked at the gap between what I know as a specialist and what my clients don't know about the same topic. At the same time, I'm frequently reminded, when I play in their world, how much they know about their own world and how often I just don't have a clue.

Please don't shirk your duties here. A good blog can be the platform for a lot of great things—including future articles, books and even guest appearances on podcasts and invitations to write regular columns. Blogging regularly makes you a stronger writer, and that, I earnestly believe, makes you a better thinker and planner.

COMBINE BLOGGING WITH EMAIL BLASTS

Don't let your blogging efforts stand alone—combine it with an occasional (twice a month is fine) email blast to your original list of people, and anyone else who has subscribed directly on your site.

What I do is very simple: I take the first three or four paragraphs of my latest blog posting and use it as a teaser in the email, then link to the blog posting itself (this way I can track how many visitors I'm getting from the effort).

I add other information to the email, such as any events I'm going to that might also interest my subscribers, interesting tidbits that I pick up (mostly links to my blog where they can read about it there—I'm always driving folks back to me web site), and announcements about teleseminars, tip sheets, and upcoming workshops that I've developed.

Wait! Did I say workshops? Yes, I did! Well, I haven't talked about those yet, but they can really add a lot of oomph to your marketing program, so let's talk about them.

DEVELOP A HALF-DAY WORKSHOP

By the time you close in on your first 90 days, you should have done at least one (if not two or three) teleseminars based on the efforts of your marketing system. In fact, by this point, with that system going and with all the content you're absorbing every week, you should be ready to develop a half-day workshop.

Why a workshop? Because it easily builds an incredible amount of credibility. A workshop is a great way to present information that is useful, relevant, and focused enough to benefit a focused audience. A good workshop can be delivered at a conference, as part of a lecture series with other speakers and trainers, or at an organization's offices.

Done right, all you need to put on a good workshop is a laptop-based presentation (I prefer Keynote, but PowerPoint works well here too), some handouts, a good speaking style, and a willing audience.

Why half-day? Because a one- or two-hour presentation is generally too short for any substantive talk, and a full-day (or multi-day) format is just too logistically complicated for most folks just starting out in business. A half-day workshop gives you four hours, with one break in the middle, to deliver your content. You normally don't have to worry about a formal meal, as most people would be happy to have snacks and coffee. Four hours is also about the time you need to deliver good information on a single topic without seeming either shallow (on the one hand) or over-the-top detailed (on the other).

You probably have a lot of questions about doing a workshop, and the first one is probably "What's the point?" Well, let's go back to my formula of credibility + visibility. A workshop, done right (and I'll explain that in a minute) can boost your credibility enormously. Whenever I give my Writing for the Web workshop, I always get a lot of interest in my services. It doesn't matter if I give it at a conference or at a corporate HQ.

Workshops also give you a lot of visibility—you can put out a press release about them, blog about how you developed it (or when you're giving one), mention upcoming dates when you network, announce your workshop in the local business journal and events calendars.

Here's something else that's great about a good workshop: it gets you out in front of your prospect base. Not only is it an opportunity for you to provide them with your expertise, it's an opportunity for you to hear directly from them. During the workshop, they will ask questions, ask for clarification, and make you aware of certain problems and issues that you would otherwise never hear about.

Now, what do I mean about putting on a good workshop? Well, it's very simple. In every single workshop I give, I use a 90-10 ratio. I only sell my services 10% of the time, and mostly that's a pitch to buy my books or visit my site. And I do it in an innovative way that is entertaining and inoffensive. The other 90% of the time, I focus on giving hard-core value to the folks who are with me.

What do I mean by that last part? Well, pedagogically speaking, I mix it up a bit. I jump in with some action items, then I back out and do a little bit of theory, a little bit of background. Then I tell them what we're going to focus on. I do a little bit more talking, and then I jump back in with the hand's on stuff.

Most of all, I use the rule of primacy to make certain things come across and stick in their minds. Primacy is a notion from psychology that illuminates some basic truths about human nature. For example, primacy indicates that most humans remember the first and last things they see/hear/experience at a workshop, and they forget the stuff in the middle.

Most folks who give a workshop don't take advantage of this fact. They start with a bunch of boring stuff at the beginning, hit the hard-core instructional meat in the middle, and then finish up with information about themselves, please visit blah-blah and call me if you need any help yada yada.

Primacy says that the audience members remember two things about this kind of presentation: the boring introduction and a hard sell. Gee, they really want to hire that guy.

I flip things around. Let me give you an example of the flow from my Writing for the Web workshop.

I start off by immediately asking each participant to write down their job description in 11 words or less. I give them five minutes to do this, meanwhile showing random pictures of my dogs and new vegetable garden—anything to lighten the mood.

We then take a look at what they've come up with, and then I slap them with a second challenge just as they're feeling good about themselves.

Can they get it down to 7 words or less?

They get another five minutes. I post pictures of a vacation or something else that's cute.

As soon as we're done there, I take them through the SO WHAT of why we did the first two exercises...how we're drowning in information, and that the gateway to successful web writing is brevity, and then I use that as a launch pad for talking about microcontent.

I illustrate that vague concept by showing them a blog post in a Web browser, then how it looks when you view it in RSS, then what that same blog post looks like once it is forwarded to someone else (it looks like an email!) and then how it looks when someone bookmarks it on Delicious or Diggs it, and then I show them how Google snaps it up and how it is trackbacked and then what it looks like on my iPhone.

In other words, in a very visual way, I show them the stakes of good (and bad!) writing while I talk about theory and information architecture. I engage them.

Very suddenly, in the middle of my discussion, I shift gears dramatically. I share my own story. Who I am, where I've come from, what I do for a living. Remember primacy? It's the middle of the talk, I don't care if they forget this stuff!

I share with them maps of my home town, show pictures of Rowdy the Roadrunner (mascot of UT San Antonio where I went to college), photos of my wife and dogs and other stuff. I show them covers of the books I've written, and my profiles on LinkedIn and Delicious and other places. Those of you who are following along are laughing, because you can see that I'm slowly rounding the corner, showing them how visible and credible I am (look at those book covers!).

Along the way I shoot out a bunch of comments on how I really feel about things—I'm not afraid to give my opinion about life, the universe, and everything. Yeah, I can be snarky and opinionated (really? shocking!) but that's part of the fun, because I'm never ever mean to anyone in the room.

We take a quick break, and when we come back, we get into the meat and potatoes of actual writing for the web. Along the way, I leave lots of time and room to entertain questions. I jump on the Web and visit participants' web sites LIVE and give them suggestions on how to improve things based on the stuff I've already showed them. It's a high-wire act that everyone gets into and keeps people laughing, thinking, and taking notes.

I've been told over and over and over again, by many participants, that my approach is unique, engaging, and fun. They recall the workshops as starting off with a bang (which it certainly does) and ending with detailed hands on material. They recall the middle portions with a chuckle (mostly because of the goofy pictures) but not a single one of them leaves the room without first getting a business card from me. They usually are the ones calling me in a week or so.

I mention all of this only because it pays to take risks, particularly if you've got something to say that comes from your values. You don't have to have a boring program that makes people fidget and wish they were having a root canal.

Now comes the caveat. I know, I hear you saying it already: "Tom, this is great, but I'm not a great speaker. I'm terrified of crowds." I understand that, I do, even though I've always been a bit extroverted and comfortable in front of groups of people. If you feel a bit awkward, you're in the majority. It isn't natural to get up in front of people.

There are two immediate cures for this problem. Find a local Toastmasters group and join them. Within six months, you'll move from bad speaker to moderately good. If you're already good, they'll make you into a master speaker. Here's another idea: sign up for a stand-up comedy or improv theater class. You may never be the next Jerry Seinfeld or Will Smith, but these classes will prepare you for anything.

What you'll find out is that you're not really afraid of talking in front of people—you're afraid of looking dumb, unprepared, or awkward in front of them. We can take care of most of that with one simple fact: **you're a ninja** in your field, right? You already know what you're talking about! All you have to do is figure out a way to package what you know in a way that can be digested by your audience.

I'm not qualified to do that for you (after all, you may have some esoteric niche focus that I've never encountered) but generally speaking, your workshop needs to address an important or pressing concern (or they won't show up in the first place), it must have a SO WHAT aspect to it (so they know they haven't wasted their time by showing up), and be hands on (to keep them from falling asleep now that they're there).

The more tangible you can make things, the better. The stronger your visuals, the better. The more you inject your values, your verve, your mojo, and your point of view, the better. Always tie it back to the SO WHAT, and always make 'em laugh or smile, and you've got a winning combination.

The final goal of the workshop is to get more business. If you do your job, you'll get that in spades. Even if you don't walk out with any project offers right there, rest assured that folks will be talking about you, emailing others about the workshop, blogging about it, and more. Double or triple that if you're at a big conference or other gathering. Just keep doing what you're doing, because you're building something great, and that never happens overnight.

FOR THE TRULY AMBITIOUS

Once you've given your workshop a few times, sit down and create either an e-book or taped presentation based on it. The taping isn't that hard—if you do it at a conference, you'll likely be taped anyway. If you have a Mac, you can add an audio track to your Keynote presentation (I'm sure you can do the same on Windows, but I have no idea how to do this).

It's up to you to give this material away for free or charge for it. It's up to you. My first inclination is to sell it, but you may want to give it away (or at least a part of it) as a promotional item for the workshop itself.

At the very least, you can take your workshop material and create an original blog post series out of it. Depending on how you do it, you can get as few as three posts or as many as ten, spaced out over various weeks. Add audio and video and supporting materials, really make a big deal out of it, and you'll see people reacting well to it.

CHAPTER 6: THE SIX-MONTH POINT

At this point, you've been in business six months. Congratulations, you've made it a lot further than a lot of folks. Usually, those folks who weren't really interested in long-term freelancing or consulting have now been able to safely go back to a full-time job or other situation. To these folks, freelancing or consulting was a way to pay the bills until something a little more stable came along. There's nothing wrong with that, believe me—the first three or four years in business, I used what I called the "six month sanity check" to figure out where I was.

For you, the six-month point gives you a very big opportunity to assess everything you've been doing and see if it makes sense to keep doing it. There's nothing wrong with doing an assessment, especially if you keep the frequency down to twice a year. What I'm going to teach you are a few rules of thumb that will help you make a good assessment of your current situation and how to respond in such a way that things get back on track (if you've gone off the rails) or stay on track (if you're doing all right).

One quick note before we continue: **you're going to keep working your system while you assess your situation**. The only difference is, you will use the results of your assessment to make course corrections to your plan and its execution. Whatever the results of your assessment, feel good about the fact that it will help guide you to the one-year mark.

HOW TO ASSESS WHAT'S GOING ON

To make a solid assessment, you're going to need a quiet afternoon (I usually pick a Saturday or Sunday away from phones, emails, instant messages, family, friends, and TV), some hard copies of your financials and business plan, the details of your system, your project histories, and some blank sheets of paper.

Assess your Marketing System

The first thing you're going to do is make a quick assessment of how many leads you're generating via your marketing system. How many folks have downloaded your tip sheet(s)? How many of those have gone on to sign up for your teleseminars? How many have gone through the one-on-one process? Of those, how many have become clients? What dollar amounts are we talking about? What kind of percentage are we talking about as compared to the rest of your revenue-generating activities?

What about your other marketing efforts? How many blog posts have you written? How many comments are you getting? When you do a search on Google for everyone linking to your blog, how many incoming links are out there?

What other credibility- and visibility-building activities are you involved in? What kind of business is being brought in from those sources? For example, how many jobs have you gotten from referrals and networking? What about other sources, like your workshops?

The goal here is to get a picture, good or bad, of the connection between your marketing efforts and the money related to those efforts. You will likely discover, if you've been following up on your system, that there is a strong connection between the money you earn and the marketing activities tied to them. Some other connections, like blog notoriety and revenue, will be much harder to pin down.

Don't despair even if there is just a small return on your marketing investment. Don't assume that you need to trash everything and do something else. It could be that your tip sheets aren't on the right topic. Or they might be the right topic but are being consumed by the wrong people. Or maybe your target audience has now moved on to another topic of interest, in which case you need to keep your system in place but update your tip sheets and teleseminars.

Same goes for your blogging—you may be going too negative, or offering too many posts of a certain kind (too many philosophical debates about the direction of the market, for instance) when your audience really needs content of a different nature (hand's-on how-to articles or product reviews).

Test the Business Plan

Tie what you're doing back to your original business plan. Sometimes, in the heat of the tactical moment, what's right in front of us distracts us. Now's the time to remind yourself what you're all about. Go back to that business plan and read it again. Is it still accurate?

If not, then update it, using the real data you've gathered from six months out in the trenches. Don't feel bad if this is the case. The world and the market move in strange ways, and you have to be smart enough to adapt. Those who don't adapt are just stubborn, and eventually, the stubborn will inherit nothing but disaster.

This is especially true if you worked out a business plan, no matter how based in reality, that didn't account for something valuable you discovered in the first six months. For example, you might have thought you wanted to code Java for a living, but later discover that you're having more fun (and making more money) being a Rails coder.

If you're making a whole lot of money and its easy work, then update the business plan! No need to be a slave to your plan if something else is working just fine and you're happy with it!

If you read your business plan and are slapping yourself in the forehead because you've strayed from your central focus, don't worry! It happens to all of us. Get back on track. Reorient yourself to your target market. Reacquaint yourself with your core values and how you expressed them. It's okay—we all get distracted.

Review the Project Histories

When you look at your project histories, divide the projects into two main groups—those you enjoyed working on and those you didn't enjoy working on. Of the ones you did enjoy working on, were you happy with all aspects of the project work? For example, was the fee high enough, were the clients to your liking, was the work interesting? Make notes of what you liked and didn't like in this first group.

Next, move on to the ones you didn't enjoy working on. Why didn't you enjoy these? Was the pay too low? Clients not a good fit? Was the work boring? You have to know why you didn't like the jobs. There may be some things you can salvage (like avoiding a certain type of client) but first you have to make an unemotional assessment.

Knowing why you like something (or don't like something) is a powerful tool—it helps you build a model or framework for future success. If you look at your project histories and discover that you really enjoy doing JavaScript work but are underbidding each job so much that you hardly can afford to do them, then you have some pretty good evidence that you'd better raise your rates.

I used a similar process to discover that what I really enjoyed to do was speaking and writing—those were the two activities that gave me the highest enjoyment and the highest profit. Unfortunately, my assessment showed that they were only 20% of my business. The other 80% was spent doing things I really didn't enjoy doing. So I made a bold move and methodically rearranged my business to focus on the things I loved to do. In six months, I had a much more balanced work life and my revenues and profits were up.

You may discover some puzzling or unsettling patterns as a result of looking at your project histories. You might, for example, discover that you keep ending up with clients that jerk you around financially. You know the type—they bounce checks, forget to pay deposits on time, and so on. You have to realize that when patterns like this emerge, the one common denominator is **you**.

You're the one who puts up with it.

You're the one who enables it by not saying anything or setting ground rules.

You're the one who must enjoy it, because you keep doing it.

Once you detect a pattern that you don't like, it's up to **you** to respond to it. Perhaps you put in a policy of not doing work until the deposit check clears. Maybe you develop some clarity around the kinds of clients you'll work with. Remember that not responding is also a response—it means that you don't want to do anything about it, so you have no right to complain when bad things happen.

During one such six-month review, I discovered that 7 of my 10 current clients shared the same general characteristics:

1. They were nit-picky to a fault.
2. They called and emailed at odd hours and expected a response immediately.
3. They mucked me around when it came to financial matters.
4. They never had their act together but expected me to respond to emergencies.
5. They were nasty people with bad personalities.

I was so stressed and so bewildered by my situation that I took two extreme actions to get out of it:

1. I raised my rates by 30% overnight, which caused four of these clients to go away forever.
2. I developed a five-part filter for identifying these kinds of clients in the future.

When the four clients left, I thought my life was over. Surely my business would tank and never recover. Wrong. With those four gone, I had a whole bunch more time for the three good clients (remember, I had seven bad ones and three good ones?) who gave me more work. They could tell I was in a better mood and had more time for their needs.

What about the other three clients? They stayed with me after I raised my rates, but they became a lot more judicious about calling me at odd hours. I had made it much more expensive for them to just pull my strings like a puppet.

The five-part filter was a really important step, because I could use it to silently evaluate a prospective client without being a jerk about it. As we sat there and interacted, I'd make sure to enact different parts of my filter, being as casual as I could possibly be. They had to pass at least four of the five filter points in order for me to want to work with them.

Here's what I came up with:

1. **Are they willing to pay a deposit?** If they aren't, or if they hem and haw, they're probably not a good choice.
2. **Do they have a deadline?** If they don't, then there's no urgency. Urgency is what makes consulting profitable.
3. **Do they have metrics for success?** They have to know what success looks like: 50% more sales, 100 new clients, whatever.
4. **Are they willing to listen?** I give away a little bit of advice even before I get hired. If they don't take my idea and at least consider it, why should I bother working with them?
5. **Are they willing to do a bit of homework?** I always ask them to do something for me— collect URLs, documents, testimonials, whatever. It's a test. If they don't do it, then I'm not likely to be interested. I'm a partner, not a slave.

Your list will be different, of course, as it will be driven by your values. Feel free to use my list as a starter, of course. The important thing is to have some kind of filter, and I mention it now only because you won't be able to develop one just out of thin air—you have to do it once you've been operating for a while. Having it for the future, though, will greatly increase your chances of creating a sane work life.

The idea of a filter may seem presumptuous to you, but it makes perfect sense to anyone who has been used and abused by crappy clients, and it's a good way to keep bad things from happening to you in the future.

Simplifying Your Work/Life with 80/20

One very important thing you can do at the six-month timeframe is to look at the revenue you're generating. Use Quickbooks (or whatever tool you're using for keeping tabs on the finances) to give you two reports. The first should be a report on the customers you have, ranked by revenue. The other should be top services you offer, ranked by revenue.

No matter how long you've been in business or what niche you're in, you're going to notice a very interesting phenomena. It's the Pareto Principle, known to you as the 80/20 rule. You'll see that 80% of your income will come from just 20% of your clients. You'll also see that 80% of your income comes from 20% of your services.

The obverse is also true—80% of your hassles will come from 20% of your clients, usually the bottom-feeding, slow-paying, angst-causing 20 percent.

Using the 80/20 rule, examine what is going on. Take a look at the 20% of clients that make up the bulk of your income. Are you happy working for them? Do you want more of these kinds of clients? Well, one way to do that is to critically examine the other 80% of your clients (the ones only bringing in a tiny bit of your income). Is it time to give these people the boot and make more room for better clients?

What about the 20% of services that bring in 80% of the income? Are you really happy doing those things? Are they profitable? Will they lead to better things? Or are you stuck doing a bunch of things you'd rather not be doing? The only way to know is to go through this process.

In other words, the end result of this quick analysis could very well be a shocking discovery: that you may be really busy doing stuff you hate, for clients you don't care to work for. It's okay, I went through the same thing—and I worked hard to change it instead of just sitting there in a rut.

Or you might be lucky enough to find out that you're doing just what you want to do for just the right clients. If that's the case, good for you, just keep right on going!

The 30% Rule

One more thing before we close out this chapter. I want to talk about the kind of mistake you only make once, mostly because it can kill off your business if you fall prey to it. I did fall prey to it, but somehow I pulled out of the nosedive it caused—but it took me months to recover and get back to a semblance of prosperity.

What am I talking about? Something that's easy to do, but not so easy to recognize as a problem: putting too many eggs in one basket.

Take a look at the revenue report by client. Undoubtedly you'll notice that just a small percentage (20% or so) do bring in the lion's share of the revenue—that's pretty much universally true.

However, one thing that can spell doom is having a single client with an unnaturally large percentage of total revenue. Early on, I was working almost exclusively for a giant Fortune 100 company, writing articles, case studies, and all kinds of other stuff for them. I was doing some other consulting and web development off to the side, but this big client easily accounted for half (or more) of my revenue stream.

Everything was fine for a year and a half. Great relationship, lots of work, lots of bills being paid.

Then one day, I got a call from my contact. The company was shutting down all projects for the foreseeable future, effective immediately. No explanations, no warnings, slam-bam thank-you ma'am, it's time to roll up the carpets and leave. I had three little projects going that stopped mid-stride. I was able to send in those invoices and got partial payments, plus I had two or three other payments coming in from previous invoices.

I was left stranded, and the only person I could blame was myself. I immediately went to work drumming up new business (I didn't have a marketing system, so I made hundreds of cold calls) and it took several months to get back up to my previous revenue levels.

Fifteen months later, without any explanations, the three-letter Fortune 100 giant came back and rehired me for some contract work, but this time, I'd already put in a policy—never have more than 30% of my revenue from a single source. I've only broken that policy once since then, and that's when I landed a $250,000 consulting gig out of the blue with another Fortune 100 giant, which accounted for 60% of my income that particular year (hey, stuff happens!).

Is 30% an amount I arrived at via some rigorous scientific method? Nope. It's just a hunch, a gut-feel, that I shouldn't have any one entity have more than a third of my entire business (and by extension, my health and well-being) in the palms of their hands. You may have a different number (like 20% or 40%) but no matter what, you'd better have a number.

The reason? No client is forever. Economic tides roll in and then roll out just as quickly. CEOs and VPs and managers come and go. Theories and practices ebb and flow. One day, it's all PHP. The next day, it's Ruby on Rails. Then back again. The only way to build true security is through diversification.

A Quick Note

No two businesses grow and evolve the same way. There's a nice little myth out there that says that when they succeed, their revenues all grow straight up and to the right. That they all go from one-man shops to multinational corporations. That it's suspect if you stay small, or focus only on one niche.

Don't believe that myth. Your business is yours, and yours alone. Yes, you have to take care of the fundamentals, but you'll have times when business is booming, and times when your business feels like a dead weight around your neck. There will be times when you get up every morning with joy in your heart, and other times when you just hate the thought of going into the office. There will be days when you can't imagine doing anything else for the rest of your life, and days in which you polish the resume and talk to recruiters because you can't stand dealing with suck head clients who don't pay their friggin' bills.

This is all normal. The key thing here is to realize that you don't have to grow your business the way everyone else has. You're free to do what you want. You can pass up certain opportunities, or pursue others that make sense only to you.

One thing's for sure: you need a plan to get you to 3, 5, 7, or 10 years, just like you needed a plan to take the leap. Just keep assessing yourself every six months, but keep on keeping on. Keep the system running.

Chapter 7: The One-Year Mark

Happy Birthday! You've been in business one year. Depending on where you live, your niche, your marketing efforts, and the economic times, your first year can range from "pure struggle" to "outstanding" or somewhere in between. No matter what, you'll probably remember your first year in business for the rest of your life, because most of the problems, issues, and challenges that dog you throughout your career will happen in those first 365 days.

If you've made it this far, it's time for a second six-month evaluation. This time, you're not just going to take the pulse of your current business (where your money is coming from, who your best clients are, what marketing activities are the most effective), you're also going to start looking around for opportunities to diversify and grow your business.

If you're anything like me, you'll hit your one-year mark, create an annual revenue report, make a pot of coffee, and sit down somewhere quiet to go over the numbers. Now, anyone who knows anything about doing this kind of analysis will tell you that what you need is a bookkeeper to hold your hands through all the reports and analysis, that a mere mortal could never do a good enough job.

Codswallop, I tell you! Codswallop! As a business owner, you need some kind of fluency and familiarity with financial analysis. In this section, I'm going to give you the bare-bones basics, because you only need to know a little bit to keep the ship moving in the right direction.

About 10 minutes after you start your initial glance at the financials, you're going to glance at the number at the bottom of the income report and you're going to have two reactions:

"I can't believe I made that much money!" This is almost always the first reaction from someone who has only been a W-2 employee without any real visibility as to how money is made in this world of ours. You'll feel a certain amount of pride that you were able to make every single one of those dollars (or yens, pounds, or euros) that have come into your life.

This feeling of elation is usually followed by: "I can't believe I worked so hard for so little money!" It's also a natural reaction, one that stems from having worked 800, 1000, 1200, or 1400 billable hours and realizing that no matter how hard you work, there really are only so many billable hours in a year (or if you're on a project fee basis, only so much time for working on projects).

I started my business in May 2001, so my first year in business included the horrendous events of 9/11. My wife was living in New York City at the time (attending cooking school—we moved her into a Manhattan apartment two days before the planes hit the towers), and let me tell you, it was a sub-optimal time for focusing on business to say the least. That first year in business was tough, and so was the second, because 2002 wasn't much better.

Still, when I did the numbers that first year, in May 2002, I realized that I'd earned about $70,000. That may not sound like much once you subtract all the expenses, but back then I was blown away by the fact that I'd brought in anything at all, considering how badly the economy tanked after 9/11 and how bad the first three months of 2002 really were. It was also amazing to note that this number wasn't much lower than the base salary I'd had at my corporate job the previous year.

I immediately realized that any goal was achievable and that all I had to do to succeed was reach out and grab what I wanted. I set a higher goal for the next year — six figures or bust!—and went after it with a grim determination. I didn't really know what I was doing yet, but I worked very long hours (20 hour days, six or seven days a week for months on end) and indeed, I hit that six-figure mark by summer 2003, and then sustained that performance for the next five years running.

However, I began to notice something, and it didn't make me very happy: if I stopped working for any reason (i.e., took a trip or vacation) I stopped making money. I also noticed that my body physically couldn't cope beyond a certain number of work hours. In fact, when I looked at several years' worth of records, I noticed that my income at 1600 billable hours per year wasn't that much different from my income at 1500 or even 1400 billable hours. I may have added 100 more hours, but I really didn't add that much more to my revenue. And I certainly didn't have that much more security in terms of ongoing revenue streams.

So I set out to achieve two goals: grow my business (by hiring), and diversify my income, in that order. It's the order that people normally tackle these things, because that's what all the books and business coaches say the order should be. I wish I'd done it the other way around, because I'd have been a happier person for it, and a lot more productive and focused to boot.

So here's what I'm going to do: I'm going to pass on yet more hard-won wisdom. If you ever have the opportunity to a) grow your business or b) diversify your income, always choose diversification first. There's always time to grow your business, but once it grows, you start to focus on all those things that have nothing to do with income-generating activities. Instead, you start dealing with HR issues, and taxes, and permits, and landlords, and rental insurance, until one day you find that only 10% of your day is spent dealing with customers.

Are you ready? Let's learn about diversification.

DIVERSIFY YOUR INCOME FIRST

At some point, even the most die-hard workaholic freak (i.e., someone just like me) will work so much that they hit a wall. It happened for me at the end of year 6. I'd worked myself into a lather. Even into my fourth year of business, 12-hour days were routine. So were "working weekends." Forget "real" vacations—that was for sissies. At some point, in 2004, my wife and I took a long weekend down at the beach, but I took my laptop and smart phone to stay in touch. Work, work, work.

But you start noticing something important: the more you work, the flatter the income curve. Oh sure, at first, your income shoots up as you put in the hours. But very soon, it flattens out, and it takes a whole bunch of hours, time you'll never ever get back, to increase your revenue stream.

There's one universal law of physics that you will never escape: there are only so many billable hours in a year, only so much time left over from sleeping, bathing, eating, socializing and resting to actually work on projects and still be fresh enough to do good work. Most folks say that 2000 hours is a maximum amount of time you can spend on work in a year (40 hours x 50 weeks) and that's pretty accurate on the surface, but the reality is that your income-generating hours will be far less than that. That's because in any given week, you're going to have many hours devoted to non-billable work—remember, you've got to run down to the office supply store, return phone calls, attend meetings, fax documents, make copies, work on taxes, and so on.

At first, you'll be lucky to get 5-10 billable hours per week. Later on, you'll hit a practical maximum of 20-25 hours per week unless you end up with some kind of on-site contracting gig, in which case you'll still have to do other pesky things besides your "real work." Things like managing email, bookkeeping, etc.

If you consider 20 hours a week a good average, we're talking 1000 hours a year. At $100/hour (to keep the math simple) you're talking about $100,000. That's if you work those hours. If you get sick, or need a break, or get distracted by something, you might not make that much.

The mistake that most people make is to go out and hire someone to help them out with things. I want you to put the brakes on—there's always time to grow your business, especially if it's successful. What we want to try first is a little bit of income diversification.

The best thing you can do as a consultant is to create a line of information products. You already have a blog, and hopefully you've been keeping up with your teleseminars and workshops, which means that you have a couple of valuable things: organized information, and an audience.

When you do your teleseminars, you're recording them. I want you to take those recordings (pick the best four or five teleseminars you've done in the past year) and create an audio series. Using tools such as GarageBand (or other audio editing tools) turn those teleseminar recordings into something that your audience would find valuable and compelling. Perhaps its a series of teleseminars on improving their online marketing, or doing a better job of database administration, or whatever it is you're an expert on.

Create an account on ClickBank (it costs about $50 to become a seller) and offer the audio series for sale via that site—they'll handle all the merchant stuff for you. Make sure that you give the 250,000 affiliates in the program a chance to prosper by reselling your information—offer them a 30%, 40% or 50% cut of each sale if they promote your audio program.

Why so much? Because they will reach out to all their people and bring you 100x, 200x, even 500x what you could do on your own. Giving up half your revenues is nothing once you consider that you've brought in 100 times more business (or more) than you could ever drum up yourself.

You're also going to blog about your new product—making sure that everyone on your RSS feed picks up on the announcement. You'll write a press release and send it out via PrWeb.com. You'll also send out an email to let folks know about your new information product. Use a headline or subject line that is informative and newspaper-like: "Top 10 Ways to Secure Your Web Site" or whatever it is you're talking about. Use body copy that is informative and tells folks how to purchase your product. Steer clear of the hype-filled communications that you see every day on the web.

The goal here is not to get rich overnight, but to get rich eventually. That's a big difference, thanks to changing out one word. In fact, with your first product, you need to think reasonably small. I always tell folks that I want my information product to bring in $100 a day. If my audio program or e-book can do that, then that means and extra $3,500 or so in my pocket every year. That's revenue that comes in without my having to work for it.

After you have the audio program out there and launched, follow up with a new information product a few weeks later. This time, put together an e-book that consists of 20 or 30 blog posts on a single topic or series. Don't worry that folks won't purchase it because it was first offered for free on the blog. Ours is a society that spends a billion dollars a year on bottled water. In other words, they pay for packaging. Your stuff has more business value than water, right?

So go through your blog posts. Are there 15-20 blog posts that could make a 40-50 page e-book on a single topic? How about your top 30 blog posts by visitor traffic? How about the top 30 blog posts in terms of comments received? Or the most popular blog posts in terms of incoming links?

Package them together with a snappy title, market it through Click2Sell, and repeat the process. Then do it again a few weeks later, using audio or e-books or even a video presentation (making a screencast series for those of you with a penchant for how-to content is a good angle). Don't stop until you have 8-10 products out there—this will take you between 3 and 6 months.

Don't forget that information products aren't just e-books or audio programs! Software also counts, and software comes in all shapes an sizes, from dedicated widgets to full-on software-as-a-service type offerings. Don't forget that more and more of us are working from devices, so selling things like iPhone applications is just as good a business model as creating stuff that runs on web servers.

Eventually, one of three things will happen.

1. You will build a side business selling information products. This business will soon have the potential of eclipsing your "main" business, but

the best part is that you can run this business pretty much on autopilot. If you go on vacation, your products will still sell, and you'll get a check. If you want to cut back on the consulting, that's okay, the products will still sell, you'll still get paid.

2. You will build a reputation as someone who knows what they're talking about, because there will be so much stuff out there with your name on it. Your blog, your e-books, your teleseminars and audio programs, your workshops, and all the rest will build a personal brand that is highly CREDIBLE and highly VISIBLE.

3. You will have the best of both worlds: passive income and reputation building. Enough said about that, just about anyone on the planet can see why this would be a good thing for a technical consultant.

One very important step that people often miss in this little game of building incremental value: start adding links to your products everywhere. Your blog needs to link to your products. Any email blasts to your subscriber list needs to have at least one ad for a related information product (the key here is the "related" part—don't just throw in random references). Mention in your official bios provided with submitted articles, press releases, and speaking engagements that you're the guy who created such and such an e-book or audio podcast.

If you've got two e-books out there, make sure that the last page of each e-book links to where you can buy the other. Mention the e-books in related teleseminars and workshops. Remember, if the product is related to what folks are reading, seeing, hearing, or experiencing, then they won't mind that you bring it up.

With just a little bit of time, and not a lot of expertise, you can grow a complex web of cross-selling that will lead to more passive income in your business. Every dollar you make in this way is a dollar you didn't technically have to work for—and in fact, you'll get to the point where you put in a dollar's worth of effort and get back ten, fifteen or a hundred dollars in sales over the lifetime of the product offering.

OKAY, NOW GROW YOUR BUSINESS, IF YOU MUST

Once you have some income diversification in place, you can start thinking about growing your business. By growing, I mean "hiring some help." But you're not going to take the traditional route by any means. You haven't up to this point, so why start now, right?

The first prerequisite to "hiring help" is having enough work for the help. This is an important point that is all too often overlooked by most people. New business owners assume that just being busy is enough of an indication to go out and hire. Wrong! You may be busy because you're terribly disorganized, or because your clients cause you to do the daily run-around. So before you do anything as minor as bringing in some kind of help, you really need to be sure you have enough work to keep that freelancer busy.

The traditional route says that you should hire full-time staff until you have the talent on hand to take care of project needs. This approach assumes that you'll be able to keep business going at current (or higher levels). However, recent history indicates that we really don't have that kind of control. No matter how masterful we are at business, we can't control the budgetary processes at a Fortune 100 company, right? We certainly can't control things like wars, stock market downturns, and other bits of nastiness that could send your fortunes down the tubes if you're out there trying to carry a bunch of payroll overhead.

So the first thing you're going to do is to grow your business with the help of others. You're going to do that by first partnering with other freelancers and consultants in those areas where you need help. Need a copywriter, designer, or CSS expert? Find someone you can trust to work together with you. It doesn't matter what the arrangement is (you're the main contractor, he/she is the main contractor, or you're equals being paid separately) as long as you're both sharing the pains and gains.

Let me be clear when I define "partner." This isn't some kind of contractual partner thing, as in "partners in a business." This is a more temporary, autonomous arrangement, as in "partners in crime." Just want to be clear here. Oh, and don't do anything criminal, 'kay?

The next step up from partnering is to subcontract. My preference used to be to subcontract folks on my own, but lately I've been using technical contracting agencies for specialists (they vet the candidates, provide them with timekeeping, deal with HR issues, and so on) and temp agencies for office help (they can find folks who work part-time if that's all you need, plus lots more that's good). Subcontracting agencies already have negotiated rates, so all you have to do is make sure that you get your profit in there as well—I've found that you have to add at least 25% or 30% on top of what the contractor (or agency) is making to make it worthwhile.

So if you're charging the customer $100, the maximum you can pay a contractor is $70 or $75 an hour. If you're working with agency contractors, you're likely paying that amount to the agency, which will also have its own 30% fee (at the very least—I know of a few who charge an extra 50%), so the contractor in this case ends up walking away with $50 and hour.

The only time I hire someone on as a W-2 employee these days is when it gets so big and complicated that I can't avoid it. I haven't had anyone on my payroll (besides myself) for 16 months since I made my decision to rescale my business. I had W-2 employees for three years previous to that, and only contractors and partners the two years before that.

The only reason I went with employees is simple: it became harder and harder to find quality contractors who could devote their attention to my needs. In other words, the only way I could 100% guarantee that my projects were being worked on was to offer them a 40-hour-per-week job, a desk, a computer, and the pleasure of my company. In exchange, I get to add the complexity of payroll withholdings and taxes (once you hit six employees, the cost of payroll administrivia is like having a bum just hanging around doing nothing but taking up space), medical coverage (we offered basic coverage to our people) and the joys of HR squabbles every day.

What happened very quickly is that I had to make the shift from entrepreneurial consultant (with a keen eye for analyzing a customer's problem and offering a solution) to manager (in which I totally sucked at the empathy game you have to play with people who are working for you). Many of my consultant friends, most of them actually, including myself, have a pretty hard time with this kind of switch.

The reason is simple: you got into this game to work with customers. You live for the white boarding sessions, the back and forth, crafting solutions to intractable problems. Once you have employees, the enemy begins its remorseless advance. At first it is just little things, like setting up direct deposit and little withholding things here and there, so you hire a part-time bookkeeper and a payroll service. Then its grows into more and more meetings to keep things on track, and eventually it gets to the point where you almost need a full-time people manager to deal with personalities and issues—doubly so if you suck at people management, which is probably very true of at least some of the technical folks reading this right now.

You end up having days like I did, where you spend four hours making the peace when one employee, valiantly trying to quit smoking but cutting back to one or two a day, is being harangued by another employee who successfully quit and sees the other's failure as some kind of moral ineptitude. So instead of making money or meeting with clients, you become a parent.

There are those of you who are reading this and are shaking your heads, saying "Gee, that's not how you handle that situation, you're just not good at managing people!" And I would totally agree. That's why I had retool my business, get back to basics, and get away from the model that said that growth was the only way to succeed. All I'm saying, in my own long-winded, anecdotal way, is "Don't you believe it!"

Always, always, always try income diversification first. You'll end up with six or seven tidy little passive income resources without adding to your management overhead. Later on, when it becomes too stressful to keep track of all the checks you're depositing, hire a nice young person to come help you.

Conclusion

You now know more than enough to survive and thrive in your new career. Follow the plan, and you will get steady work from a growing list of clients. With any luck, they will be the kind of clients you love, and the work will bring you joy and fulfillment.

Since, I don't believe in long, teary goodbyes, I'm going to close this short book with three brief things:

1. Learn to give back to your community.
2. Follow what's going on at this book's companion blog.
3. Check out some resources for your future edification.

Giving Back

Giving back is a topic that's near and dear to my heart. I make sure that every year, I donate my time and energy to at least one group, or make a charitable donation, or something like that. For example, as a runner, I will have my company pay for me to run in local 5K and 10K races that benefit a specific cause. I sit on the board of the Austin chapter of the American Marketing Association (I do a lot of business with marketing professionals). I donate my skills and time to at least one non-profit group (sometimes two).

I don't do this to be a saint, mind you—I'm not.

I do it because it isn't just about the money. It's about my reputation. I want to do a little bit of good in this world, and if setting up a blog for a medical charity or donating a $100 to a literacy program or running for the cure adds to that goodness, then so much the better.

I know it's a lot to think about, and that's why I only mention it at the end of the book (you should be well on your way to steady income by now), but find some time to get involved with some pro-bono activity. Don't do it at the very beginning as a "way to get your name out there"—the only name you'll get is as sucker who does stuff for free. No, wait until you've got a steady client roster, then fish around for good organizations that need your help and can bring you the kind of VISIBILITY you want. Or just do it to feel really good about yourself.

Don't make a big deal about it, by the way. This isn't some kind of contest in which we all strive to "do well by doing good." Any kind of promotional activity around this kind of giving back will just negate all your good karma. Just do what you do and make sure the right people know what you're about and what you've done. The rest will take care of itself, particularly if you have a system in place to capture new business.

CHECK OUT THIS BOOK'S COMPANION BLOG

I'll keep this brief. I've started a blog over at http://www.myerman.com in which I've started posting articles and other information on technical freelancing and consulting. Come join in the fun by commenting on what's out there. If you want to write for that blog, let me know, I'd love to have you on board, particularly if you've got something meaningful to share.

Watch the blog space for a future announcement about a coaching service—I'm still working out the details, but the plan is to have a "mastermind group" that meets weekly to help folks get over the wall. The first group will focus on the first year in business, naturally, but as time goes on, other needs will likely emerge. More details to follow!

SOME GREAT BOOKS YOU NEED TO READ

Frequently, I get asked what are some of my favorite business books. I got tired of sending out emails (which rapidly went out of date as books went out of print), so I set up a Listmania list over at Amazon.com. Every once in a while, I add (or delete) a book from the list, but I'm sending everyone over there.

So, instead of offering you a static list here in this printed book, I give you a link to a living, breathing list of resources. Isn't the Web just grand?

Because the Amazon.com URL is so convoluted, I've created a TinyURL for it, here it is:

http://tinyurl.com/5g3j7c

Go ahead and check the list out. I particularly like *The E-Myth Revisited* (it really changed a lot of my basic assumptions about business) and *Getting Business to Come To You*. If you have books you want to add to the list, feel free to drop me a line:

tom@tripledogs.com

I hope you've enjoyed the book, and that it brings you much success in your endeavors.

www.ingramcontent.com/pod-product-compliance
Lightning Source LLC
Chambersburg PA
CBHW051219200326
41519CB00025B/7180